Disney
PRINCESS
Healthy Treats

INSIGHT
EDITIONS

San Rafael • Los Angeles • London

Disney PRINCESS

Healthy Treats

By Ariane Resnick, CNC

INSIGHT
EDITIONS

San Rafael • Los Angeles • London

Contents

Chapter 4 Shareable Entrées

Chapter 5 Handheld Treats

Chapter 6 Dessert Shareables

Chapter 7 Sippables

Introduction

Ever since Snow White made her debut on the silver screen back in 1939, the Disney Princesses have enchanted audiences across the globe, inspiring us to be our best selves, chase our dreams, and find joy in the everyday, even if it means whistling while we work to help pass the time. From Jasmine's generosity to Ariel's free-spirited curiosity to Rapunzel's never-ending creativity, the Disney Princesses are always there to encourage us all to embrace the Princess within each of us.

One of the most important aspects of being a Princess is taking care of our bodies and fueling ourselves with a balanced and healthy diet. While eating our fruits and veggies may not seem very exciting, it's easy to discover that there are many ways to make what we eat both tasty and healthy by adding sneaky healthful ingredients—such as avocados, applesauce, or coconut oil. These ingredients can reduce the amount of sugar and fat content in beloved sweet treats and comfort foods.

Within this book, each Disney Princess inspires a unique and vibrant flavor in the appetizers, snacks, entrées, drinks, and desserts presented. Together, we celebrate the different cultures of the Princesses, learning how to make delicious recipes such as a traditional Scottish stew (p. 76) that Queen Elinor may have served to Merida, and a Black Sesame Custard Tart (p. 103) that Mulan might have shared with her father.

Everyone benefits from eating healthier—princesses included! This book aims to help you do that in a way that's fun, festive, and delicious. While the recipes in this book may contain some ingredients that are less familiar to you, none of the techniques involve any special skills. With the tips on the following pages, you'll be well on your way to creating Disney Princess-inspired healthful treats in a safe, efficient manner. Enjoy!

Cooking and Baking Tips

Dress safely. If you have long hair, tie it back so it doesn't get in the way. If you have anything dangly on your clothes, tuck it away or change into something that doesn't. Wear an apron to save your own clothes if you'll be doing anything messy with fruit, oil, or any other ingredient that can stain.

Wash your hands well before beginning any kitchen project. No one wants cookies with cat hair in them! It's also helpful to wash your hands after touching anything messy, before moving on to the next step of a recipe.

Exercise caution with any sharp tools, especially knives. If a chop or dice is too risky, let an adult take care of it. Always err on the side of caution if you're worried about a technique being too advanced.

Stay put. If you have anything on the stove, do your best to remain in the room to prevent dishes from boiling over or burning. If you're baking something in the oven, set a timer so you know to return when it's done.

Stay cool. Use thick, fully dry pot holders to pull dishes out of the oven or off the stove. Set baking dishes down on a trivet instead of directly on the counter. And while tasting is a fun activity, save it for safe temperatures. Let finished dishes cool first, and if you're tasting a recipe midway through, remove a small amount from the pot or pan and let it cool for a few minutes before trying it.

Healthier Ingredients and Dietary Terms

Eating more healthfully should be both comfortable and feasible for you. To that end, all specialty ingredients used in this book are available online and at health food stores, if you can't find them at your local grocery store. Let's take a look at the ways this book accommodates dietary restrictions, and what basic ingredients you might like to have on hand to make the recipes.

Sugar-Free Sweeteners

In this book we substitute some of the refined sugar in sweets for natural sweeteners that don't affect blood sugar. Generally, we use a ratio of substituting out one-third of the sugar in a recipe for a lower-sugar alternative. That way it isn't noticeable at all! If you find that you don't mind the taste of natural, noncaloric sweeteners, you can certainly choose a bigger ratio, like 50:50 each. Granulated sweeteners are interchangeable, and you can choose whichever you like best. The most common cup-for-cup options are:

Swerve: This is a favorite because in addition to its main ingredient, erythritol, it contains nutrients that help it bake up better and more like sugar.

Allulose: This sweetener comes in second because it has no aftertaste and a mild flavor similar to sugar.

Monk fruit: Also sold as Lakanto, this sugar-free option melts easily.

Erythritol: The main component of Swerve mentioned above, this sweetener can have a slight cooling effect on the tongue and may crystallize when heated.

Coconut sugar: Unlike the others in this list, coconut sugar does contain calories and actual sugar. It's a less-refined version of sugar with notes of caramel flavor that is made from—you guessed it—coconut. It's available in light and dark brown; for the recipes in this book, we recommend the light version.

Stevia: In addition to cup-for-cup sugar replacements, these recipes also use stevia. It's a more concentrated sweetener, so you can't substitute some of the sugar in baking for it because you would lose volume. Many people like the taste of liquid drops more than powder. If a recipe calls for stevia to taste, use the amount you like best; try adding it drop by drop until a drink tastes just right to you.

Xylitol: This common sugar alternative isn't recommended for two reasons: It's dangerous for pets, and it has a minty, cooling effect in the mouth.

Flours

All-purpose gluten-free flours are plentiful these days, but they aren't more diverse than wheat flour (unless, of course, you have celiac disease or a gluten allergy). Because all-purpose gluten-free flours are pretty void of nutrients, we've chosen to use single, whole-food flours instead wherever possible. Each of the below flours is made by grinding a whole food into a powder. Note that unlike the sugar substitutes, these flours below are not cup-for-cup wheat flour replacements, and they can't be exchanged evenly with wheat flour in conventional recipes.

Almond flour: High in protein, almond flour is an excellent choice for mimicking the same crumb as wheat flour in baked goods. It doesn't have any binding power, so it's usually used in conjunction with another flour or a starch. In order for your recipes to look as close to the "real thing" as possible, choose finely ground almond flour that has had the skin removed so it has no brown spots.

Coconut flour: This dense flour has tons of fiber and great binding power. It absorbs liquid quickly, so be sure to follow the recipes very closely with regards to the quantity used.

Brown rice flour: Made by grinding brown rice, this flour has a slightly nutty taste. Like almond flour, it doesn't have any binding ability, so it usually isn't used alone.

Fun Fats

Not every recipe in this book requires additional fats, but it's helpful to understand why the ones chosen are used when they are. While butter is delicious and does offer some health benefits (such as vitamin A), it doesn't work for everyone, and many health advocates advise limiting its consumption. In that spirit, we have replaced it wherever possible with oils that have health-promoting benefits.

Avocado oil: For recipes in this book calling for a neutral oil, avocado oil is a top choice. It has a very light flavor, high smoke point, and tons of heart-healthy monounsaturated fatty acids.

Grapeseed oil: A more affordable option than avocado oil, grapeseed oil has a neutral flavor similar to vegetable oil and is also recommended wherever a neutral oil is called for in these recipes. It's high in antioxidant vitamin E and is a much better choice than vegetable oil, which isn't recommended for use.

Olive oil: It's old news that olive oil is one of the most health-promoting oils. This Mediterranean diet staple has a strong flavor if you use extra-virgin cold pressed. We've used light olive oil for recipes in which you don't want too much olive flavor, and extra-virgin in which you want that rich, Mediterranean taste.

Coconut oil: Though it does contain saturated fat, coconut oil has a host of health benefits that make it beloved by the natural foods world. Its medium-chain triglycerides are a good source of energy, and it can increase good (HDL) cholesterol.

Dietary Terms

Outside of just wanting to eat better in order to feel better, many people have reactions to certain foods. Because of how prominent food allergies and restrictions are, there are many special diets that people may follow. All of the recipes in this book adhere to at least one restriction, if not more. That way, as many people as possible can enjoy the treats!

Gluten Free: Gluten—a protein found in wheat, barley, rye, and some less common grains—provides all the stretch and softness we love in baked goods. Unfortunately, for people with celiac disease, gluten triggers an attack response in their bodies. Recipes in this book that say "gluten free" do not use ingredients such as wheat flour or soy sauce. Gluten-free recipes are notated as *GF*.

Refined Sugar Free: White sugar is the most common form of sugar in our food. For recipes that are refined-sugar free, we use only unrefined sweeteners. These include the noncaloric sweeteners described on page 11, as well as honey and pure maple syrup. Refined-sugar free recipes are notated as *RSF*.

Vegetarian: Recipes that don't contain any meat but do have dairy and eggs are noted as vegetarian. They're safe for a vegetarian diet without breaking any rules. Most baked goods are vegetarian by nature, so this restriction isn't a big deal in that context. Vegetarian recipes are notated as *Veg*.

Vegan: While vegetarian foods remove most animal products, vegan foods take out every one of them. Even honey is prohibited on a vegan diet, because it comes from bees. Vegan recipes have no animal products of any sort, including dairy or eggs. Because a vegan recipe is more limited than a vegetarian one, all vegan recipes in this book are also vegetarian. Vegan recipes are notated as *V*.

Low Carb: Carbohydrate, fat, and protein are the three macronutrients we eat. Some people need to avoid carbs, which come from sources such as potatoes, pasta, and sugar. Low-carb recipes are notated as *LC*.

Low Fat: Some people need to limit their intake of fat for various reasons. Fat comes from sources like butter, oil, and nuts. Low-fat recipes are notated as *LF*.

Whole Grain: When grains are either used in their original form (think brown rice) or ground whole, they qualify as whole grains. When you remove the outside hull of a grain, which is what's done for white all-purpose flour and white rice, you lose a lot of valuable nutrients. By using whole grains and whole grain flours, you can add more fiber and vitamins into your diet with minimal effort. Whole grain recipes are notated as *WG*.

CHAPTER 1

Breakfast Noshes

Aurora Overnight Oats Parfait

Aurora's sleep could only be broken by the kiss of true love. In that spirit, it takes a full night's sleep for this overnight oat parfait, which is layered with fruit and chia pudding, to chill to perfection. These parfaits keep well for days. If you're feeding multiple mouths for breakfast, you can easily double the batch.

Makes 4 parfaits

½ cup chia seeds

4½ cups milk, divided

2 cups gluten-free rolled oats

½ teaspoon salt

3 tablespoons pure maple syrup

1 cup fresh blueberries

1 cup blackberries, halved if large

4 fresh mint sprigs, optional

GF, RSF, Veg, WG

To make the chia pudding, in a mixing bowl stir together chia seeds and 2½ cups of the milk. Set aside for 10 minutes.

To make the oats, in a separate bowl stir together the remaining 2 cups milk with the salt and maple syrup. Set aside.

To assemble the parfaits, gather four pint-size Mason jars or other type of container that has a tight-sealing lid.

Layer ½ cup of the oat mixture in each jar, then top with ¼ cup of the chia pudding. Top pudding with ¼ cup each of blueberries and blackberries.

Repeat layering oats, chia, and berries until all ingredients are used, ending with berries on top. Seal tightly and refrigerate overnight before enjoying. Top with a mint sprig, if desired.

Recipe Twist

For the milk, dairy and plant-based varieties work equally well. So for a vegan parfait, substitute the milk in this recipe for a plant-based milk.

Merida Cranachan

Merida needs all the energy she can muster for her sportsmanship, and breakfast is the perfect place to start. Cranachan is a beloved Scottish dessert, but here it gets a healthful makeover fit for breakfast. Since Scottish oats aren't easily available in America, the same style can be acquired by briefly pulsing oats in a blender or a food processor. We're also using whipped yogurt rather than pure whipped cream, and lots of raspberry goodness layered in.

Makes 4 servings

- 2 cups old-fashioned rolled oats, pulsed briefly several times in a blender or food processor
- ½ teaspoon salt
- 2 tablespoons pure maple syrup
- 2 cups raspberries, fresh or thawed if frozen
- 1 tablespoon honey
- ½ cup whipping cream
- 2 cups raspberry or strawberry Greek yogurt

GF, RSF, V, WG

To make the oatmeal, add oats, 4 cups water, salt, and maple syrup to a medium saucepan; cook per package instructions.

To make the raspberry sauce, in a small saucepan combine raspberries, honey, and 3 tablespoons water. Cook over medium heat, mashing occasionally, until raspberries are broken down, about 10 minutes. Remove from the heat and let cool slightly. Use an immersion blender to blend the sauce until smooth. (Or pour the sauce into the bowl of a food processor fitted with a steel blade and process until smooth.) Strain the sauce through a fine-mesh strainer into a bowl. Refrigerate the sauce, uncovered, until ready to assemble.

To make the whipped yogurt, whip the whipping cream with an electric mixer until stiff peaks form. Slowly fold in the yogurt, then slowly fold in ¼ cup of the raspberry sauce.

To assemble, layer the oatmeal, raspberry sauce, and whipped yogurt in one large bowl or four single-serving dishes until all ingredients are used, ending with whipped yogurt on top.

Seven Dwarfs Fladle

Fladle are pancakes popular in Germany and would likely be very popular with Snow White's friends, the Seven Dwarfs, as well. Unlike the fluffy pancakes that we eat flat, fladle are thinner, like a crepe, and served in a more fun way: rolled up and sliced into thin strips. They're topped in this recipe with a compote of pear and fig—two fruits grown in Germany that can be acquired here in any season. Instead of on a plate, fladle are eaten out of a bowl.

Makes 6 servings

1 cup milk (dairy works best)

1½ cups all-purpose flour

3 large eggs

½ teaspoon salt

½ teaspoon vanilla extract

2 pears, peeled and chopped into ½-inch pieces (about 2 cups)

6 dried figs with stems removed, diced into ¼-inch pieces (about ½ cup)

½ cup apple juice or apple cider

½ teaspoon ground cinnamon, plus more for garnishing

RSF, Veg, LF

To make the pancakes, in a large mixing bowl combine the milk, flour, eggs, salt, and vanilla and whisk until smooth.

Heat a griddle or large skillet over medium-high heat and spray with cooking spray. Spoon a scant ½ cup of the fladle batter onto the hot griddle or skillet. (If using a skillet, when you add the batter lift the skillet to swirl it around, similar to making a crepe.) Cook the fladle until lightly golden on each side, about 2 minutes for the first side, and about 30 seconds for the second side. Remove the fladle from the griddle, and as soon as it is cool enough to handle, roll it up and set it aside. Repeat until all batter is used.

To make the compote, place the pears, figs, juice, and cinnamon in a medium saucepan over medium-high heat. Bring to a boil, then reduce to a simmer and cook for 10 minutes or until fruit is soft and juice has thickened.

To assemble for serving, slice each fladle into thin strips. Place a sliced fladle in a bowl, fluffing it slightly so that it looks similar to a fettuccine. Pour about ¼ cup of the compote over each serving. Sprinkle with additional cinnamon.

Jasmine Sour Cherry Smoothies

Fresh cherries can be hard to come by out of season if you aren't somewhere with a warm climate, but tart cherry juice and frozen cherries make this smoothie into something you can enjoy at any time of year. The tart juice-and-fruit combo adds an adventurous flair that bursts with flavor . . . just like Jasmine's bursting curiosity to explore her own kingdom! This easy on-the-go breakfast includes probiotic kefir, a beverage full of protein to fuel Jasmine on her travels.

Makes 1 large smoothie

½ cup tart cherry juice

1 cup plain kefir

1 cup frozen cherries

½ cup frozen banana chunks
or slices, plus more slices
for garnish, optional

1 teaspoon honey

2 ice cubes

Edible flowers, optional

GF, RSF, Veg, LC, LF

In a blender, combine the cherry juice, kefir, cherries, banana, honey, and ice cubes; blend until smooth. (This should take about 30 seconds in a high-power blender, or about 1 minute in a standard blender.)

Garnish with banana slices and edible flowers, if desired.

Recipe Twist
Because dairy kefir has much more protein than plant-based, it's the recommended option in this recipe.

Flounder Mango-and-Blueberry Striped Smoothie

Ariel's best friend, Flounder, has beautifully vibrant yellow and blue stripes. This delicious smoothie pays tribute to his stripes by alternating layers of mango and blueberries! It might sound complicated to make a layered smoothie, but it's actually surprisingly quick. It takes only 10 minutes in the freezer for each layer of this smoothie to thicken enough for the back-and-forth pouring method. Even better, you get to drink a big cup of delicious blueberries and mango.

Makes 2 smoothies

¾ cup frozen blueberries, plus more for garnish, optional

1 cup frozen banana chunks or slices, divided

⅔ cup yogurt, divided

1 cup apple juice, divided

6 ice cubes, divided

¾ cup frozen mango chunks, plus more for garnish, optional

GF, RSF, Veg, LC, LF

To make the blueberry layer, in a blender combine the blueberries and half each of the banana, yogurt, apple juice, and ice. Blend on high until smooth, then pour into a large glass and place in the freezer. Rinse out the blender.

To make the mango layer, in the blender combine the mango and the remaining half each of the banana, yogurt, apple juice, and ice. Blend on high until smooth, then pour into a large glass and place in the freezer. Freeze for 10 minutes.

To assemble the smoothie, set out two tall glasses. Take the smoothies out of the freezer and stir briefly to break up any ice chunks that may have formed. Pour 1 to 2 inches of blueberry smoothie into each glass, then pour 1 to 2 inches of mango smoothie on top of that. If they begin to meld together, pour each layer over the upturned bowl of a spoon into the cup. Continue until each glass is full and each of the smoothie layers has been used up. If desired, garnish with additional mango chunks and blueberries.

Recipe Twist

For the yogurt in this recipe, any will work: plain or flavored, Greek or regular, dairy or plant-based.

Heihei Granola Bars

While Heihei may not normally eat granola bars, he'd probably love all the ingredients in these. Since we've seen him make some questionable dietary choices—like eating a rock—this recipe should exceed his expectations. These oat-based bars are not only chock-full of great ingredients like macadamia nuts, coconut, and pineapple, they're so easy that they don't even need to be baked! They're simple enough for kids to mix together and press out with minimal supervision needed, and they keep well in the fridge for weeks.

Makes 12 granola bars

2 cups gluten-free rolled oats

½ cup almond butter

3 tablespoons pure maple syrup

2 tablespoons honey

¾ teaspoon salt

½ teaspoon ground ginger

½ cup roughly chopped macadamia nuts

½ cup roughly chopped dried pineapple

½ cup dried coconut flakes

GF, Veg

Line an 8×8-inch baking dish with parchment paper or oven-safe plastic wrap.

In a large mixing bowl combine the oats, almond butter, maple syrup, honey, salt, ginger, macadamia nuts, pineapple, and coconut flakes, and stir with a fork until fully combined. Pour onto the prepared baking dish, and press down with your hands until mixture is an even layer.

Refrigerate overnight or until firm. Cut into 12 bars. Store in the refrigerator.

Meeko Cranberry Mini Muffins

Being a raccoon, Pocahontas's friend Meeko has small hands. That means a full-size muffin might be too cumbersome for him! To make sure Meeko, who loves food and will surely want a muffin, can get his hands around these, they're made miniature—the perfect size for racoon paws and small hands. Much of the oil that you'd normally add to muffins is swapped out for applesauce, which adds fiber as well as a comforting, familiar flavor.

Makes 24 mini muffins

2 cups white whole wheat flour

⅓ cup sugar-free granular sweetener

⅔ cup sugar

½ teaspoon salt

1½ teaspoons baking powder

½ teaspoon baking soda

2 eggs

⅔ cup applesauce

½ cup orange juice

2 tablespoons neutral oil, such as grapeseed oil or avocado oil

2 cups chopped fresh cranberries or 1 cup dried cranberries

Veg, LF, WG

Preheat the oven to 375°F. Grease or spray a 24-cup mini muffin pan with cooking spray.

In a large mixing bowl whisk together the flour, sweetener, sugar, salt, baking powder, and baking soda. Make a well with the whisk in the center of the ingredients, and add the eggs, applesauce, orange juice, and oil. Whisk just until combined; do not overmix. Fold in the cranberries. Divide the batter among the prepared muffin-pan cups.

Bake until golden, about 15 minutes. Remove from the oven and let cool 15 minutes on a wire rack before serving.

Lottie Sweet Potato Pie Muffins

Tiana's friend Charlotte loves New Orleans cuisine, and sweet potato pie is a Southern classic. Here, sweet potato pie is reimagined as muffins instead. These vegan muffins are so delicious, you won't notice they have no added oil or butter. They're a filling breakfast that taste like an indulgent dessert.

Makes 12 muffins

1½ cups whole wheat flour

½ cup coconut sugar

1 teaspoon baking powder

½ teaspoon baking soda

½ teaspoon salt

1½ teaspoons pumpkin pie spice

2 cups sweet potatoes, cooked and mashed

¾ cup almond or oat milk

2 tablespoons pure maple syrup

1 tablespoon apple cider vinegar

½ teaspoon vanilla extract

RSF, V, LF, WG

Preheat the oven to 375°F. Grease or spray a 12-cup muffin pan with cooking spray.

In a large mixing bowl whisk together the flour, coconut sugar, baking powder, baking soda, salt, and pumpkin pie spice. Make a well with the whisk in the center of the ingredients, and add the sweet potatoes, milk, maple syrup, vinegar, and vanilla. Use a spatula to fold the ingredients together until combined.

Divide the batter among the prepared muffin-pan cups. Bake until golden, about 20 minutes.

Recipe Twist

If you don't have whole sweet potatoes on hand to steam or bake and mash, you can use an equal quantity of the canned variety, provided the only ingredient is pureed sweet potatoes; sweet potatoes in syrup won't work for this.

CHAPTER 2

Breaking Bread

Magic Carpet Flatbread

It's purple, yellow, and full of charm: It's not Magic Carpet (also known as Carpet), but it is a flatbread that bears a similar color scheme! Saffron and turmeric give a golden glow to this whole wheat flatbread, which is topped with a purple-hued Kalamata tapenade. The flatbread can be sliced and served as an appetizer or alongside a hearty salad for a meal.

Makes 4 flatbreads

For the flatbread

Pinch of salt

½ teaspoon ground turmeric

½ teaspoon saffron threads

¾ cup whole wheat flour

1 teaspoon light olive oil

1½ tablespoons hot water

For the tapenade

1 cup pitted Kalamata olives

2 tablespoons fresh parsley, stemmed

2 tablespoons walnuts

1 clove garlic, chopped

½ teaspoon black pepper

3 tablespoons extra-virgin olive oil

RSF, V, WG

To make the flatbread, in a medium mixing bowl whisk the salt, turmeric, saffron, and flour. Add the oil and hot water, and stir with a fork or your hand until a dough is formed. Turn the dough out onto a lightly floured surface, and continue to knead the dough until it's smooth, about 2 minutes. Roll it into a ball and set aside while you make the tapenade. If making tapenade ahead of time, let the dough rest for 10 to 20 minutes.

To make the tapenade, in a blender or food processor combine the olives, parsley, walnuts, garlic, black pepper, and olive oil. Blend or process on low until a chunky puree is formed. (Or blend until completely smooth, but some texture makes for a more interesting presentation.)

To finish the flatbread, divide the dough into four equal-size pieces, and roll out with a rolling pin into a long shape. Ideally you want a long rectangle to best resemble Magic Carpet's shape, but it's okay if the edges are rounded. Use sharp scissors to snip the short ends of the rectangle to resemble fringe.

Heat a large skillet over medium-high heat, spray with cooking spray if it isn't nonstick, and cook the flatbreads for 30 to 45 seconds on each side. They should be cooked through and have slight blisters.

To assemble the flatbread, scoop one-quarter of the tapenade onto each flatbread, spreading almost to the edges.

Pocahontas Skillet Cornbread

Squash, beans, and corn are known as the "three sisters" in Native American cuisine. While we don't know for sure what Pocahontas eats every day, these ingredients are likely an important part of her diet. Cornbread is a wonderful bread on its own, and the addition of acorn squash, kidney beans, and corn provide extra texture and protein. If you don't have a cast-iron pan, this can be baked in a greased square or round baking dish instead.

Makes 12 servings

1 cup yellow cornmeal

1 cup all-purpose flour

2 tablespoons noncaloric granulated sweetener

1 tablespoon baking powder

½ teaspoon baking soda

1 teaspoon salt

2 tablespoons honey

2 eggs

1 cup milk

⅓ cup neutral oil, such as grapeseed oil or avocado oil

½ cup cooked, mashed acorn squash

¾ cup cooked kidney beans

¾ cup fresh or frozen corn kernels

RSF, Veg

Preheat oven to 400°F.

In a large mixing bowl whisk together the cornmeal, flour, sweetener, baking powder, baking soda, and salt. Add the honey, eggs, milk, and oil to the center of the mixture, and whisk until the batter is a almost smooth. Use a spatula to fold in the squash, beans, and corn.

Pour the batter into a well-seasoned 10-inch cast-iron pan or skillet. Bake for 25 minutes, or until a toothpick inserted comes out clean. Let cool before serving.

Pumpkin Coach Cinnamon Rolls

Cinderella's coach turned into a pumpkin in the morning, but pumpkin has turned into these cinnamon rolls for a healthier twist on a classic and delicious breakfast! Pumpkin is a wonderful source of fiber and vitamin A, and coconut sugar and maple syrup are used to sweeten these rolls for unbeatable flavor. While this recipe is a natural for autumn, you can make it any time of year with canned pumpkin. Be sure to use unsweetened pumpkin puree, not pumpkin pie filling for this recipe.

Makes 12 rolls

¾ cup plus 2 tablespoons almond milk, divided

⅔ cup coconut sugar, divided

2¼ teaspoons (1 package) quick-rising yeast

¾ cup butter, divided

¾ cup canned pumpkin puree

1 egg, room temperature

2 cups spelt flour

2 cups bread flour

3 tablespoons pumpkin pie spice, divided

Pinch of salt

¼ cup plus ⅓ cup pure maple syrup, divided

4 ounces cream cheese, softened

RSF, Veg

To make the rolls, heat ¾ cup almond milk for 30 seconds in a small saucepan or in the microwave, until it reaches 110°F, or feels slightly warm to the touch. Pour it into the bowl of an electric mixer, or a medium mixing bowl if you're using a hand mixer, with ⅓ cup coconut sugar. Sprinkle the yeast on top. Melt ¼ cup of the butter and add it to the yeast mixture, along with the pumpkin puree and egg, and mix with the whisk attachment until smooth. Add spelt flour, bread flour, 2 tablespoons pumpkin pie spice, and salt. Switch to the dough hook and knead on low speed for 8 to 10 minutes. If you don't have a stand mixer, you can knead by hand on a floured surface.

Spray a large mixing bowl with cooking spray and transfer the dough ball to it. Cover it with a kitchen towel and let rise in a warm place for an hour, or until doubled in size.

Prepare a 9×13-inch baking pan with parchment paper and cooking spray. Transfer dough to a floured surface and roll into a 14×16-inch rectangle.

Combine ¼ cup butter, the remaining ⅓ cup coconut sugar, ¼ cup maple syrup, and the remaining 1 tablespoon pumpkin pie spice in a small bowl and stir them together. Spread the mixture across the dough rectangle, leaving a ¼-inch margin at the far end of the dough. Tightly roll the dough up, starting from the shorter side and finishing with the unfilled edge. Cut the roll into 12 sections using a serrated knife. Arrange the cut cinnamon rolls on the prepared baking pan. Cover with plastic wrap, and allow the rolls to rise for another 30 minutes.

Preheat the oven to 350°F. Remove the plastic wrap and bake for 20 to 25 minutes, or just until golden brown. Cool 10 minutes before frosting.

To make the frosting, in a mixing bowl combine the remaining ¼ cup butter, softened cream cheese, remaining ⅓ cup maple syrup, and remaining 2 tablespoons almond milk, and whisk until smooth. Spread over the cinnamon rolls and serve warm.

Fairy Godmother Wands

These humble breadsticks meet a dash of natural food coloring and a touch of sugar crystals, and Bibbidi-Bobbidi-Boo! This is a magic wand that any child will be delighted to play with and eat. And these magical snacks won't leave you with a pumpkin and six white mice after a few hours, either! This recipe calls for natural blue food coloring to match the fairy godmother's dress, but you can use any color you wish. Turbinado sugar, also known as Sugar in the Raw, is a minimally processed cane sugar that is sold in large crystals. It's what gives the appearance of magic sparks on these wands.

Makes 24 wands

- 2¾ cups all-purpose flour or bread flour
- 1 teaspoon instant yeast
- ¾ cup lukewarm water
- ¼ cup light olive oil, plus more for brushing dough
- 1 tablespoon honey
- ¾ teaspoon salt
- 5 to 10 drops natural blue food coloring
- ¼ cup turbinado sugar

Veg, LF

In a stand mixer bowl with the dough hook attachment, combine the flour, yeast, water, olive oil, honey, and salt. Knead for 10 minutes in the mixer, or 20 minutes by hand, until dough is smooth. With the mixer running, add the food coloring, one drop at a time, until dough reaches the desired shade. Let the dough rest for 5 minutes, then transfer it to an oiled work surface.

Shape the dough into a 14×4-inch rectangle. Brush with oil, then cover and let rest for 1 hour.

Preheat the oven to 375°F. Line two baking sheets with parchment paper.

Divide the dough into four equal pieces, then divide each piece into six strips. Roll out the strips into 14- to 16-inch wands. Brush all of them with oil and sprinkle one end with the sugar crystals, lightly pressing and rolling to allow sugar to penetrate the dough slightly.

Bake, one baking sheet at a time, for 20 to 25 minutes.

Rapunzel Challah

There are numerous ways to braid challah, but even the simplest version will be a pretty reminder of Rapunzel's beautiful bright yellow hair! That's because challah requires eggs to lend their golden glow to this loaf. The quantity of eggs in challah makes it richer in protein than most other breads. Some ways of braiding challah involve eight strands of dough, but to remind you of Rapunzel's long braid, the number in this recipe is kept to three, just like when braiding hair.

Makes 1 loaf, about 16 slices

½ cup lukewarm water

2¼ teaspoons (one package) active dry yeast

¼ cup honey, divided

4 cups all-purpose flour

2 teaspoons salt

3 large eggs

6 tablespoons neutral oil, such as grapeseed oil or avocado oil

RSF, Veg

Line a baking sheet with parchment paper. In a small mixing bowl combine the water, yeast, and 1 tablespoon honey, and stir to combine. Set aside for 5 minutes until mixture becomes frothy.

In the bowl of a stand mixer or in a large mixing bowl, mix the flour and salt. Make a well in the center and add 2 eggs, 1 egg yolk (set aside remaining egg white), the remaining 3 tablespoons honey, the oil, and yeast mixture.

Using the dough hook in a stand mixer, stir to combine then knead for 6 to 8 minutes until the dough is soft, smooth, and holds a ball shape. To do this step by hand instead, combine the ingredients then knead for 20 minutes. Cover the dough with plastic wrap and allow it to rise for 1½ to 2 hours or until doubled in size.

Transfer the dough to a floured work surface. Divide the dough into three even pieces, and form each piece into a rope about 16 inches long.

Continued on page 41

Rapunzel Challah
Continued from page 39

Connect the ends at the top and braid, putting the side pieces over the middle until all of the dough has been formed together in one braid. Place the braid on the lined baking sheet. Cover with a kitchen towel and allow to rise for 1 hour.

Preheat the oven to 375°F. Brush the challah with the remaining egg white. Bake for 30 to 35 minutes or until golden. Check the challah at 20 minutes; if it has browned too much, tent it with aluminum foil. Serve warm.

Motunui Sweet Rolls

The from-scratch version of these sweet coconut buns, known in Samoa as *pani popo*, swaps heavy cream for coconut milk, and some of the white flour for ancient grain spelt. The bulbous shape of these rolls is reminiscent of the hills of the island of Motunui, where Moana lives, and the wonderful bounty of food there. These rolls are great as a side with dinner, and the leftovers are perfect for breakfast the next day.

Makes 12 rolls

¼ cup lukewarm water

½ cup sugar, divided

2¼ teaspoons (1 package) active dry yeast

2½ cups all-purpose flour

1 cup spelt flour

1¼ teaspoons salt

One 14-ounce can coconut milk, divided

¼ cup coconut oil, melted

2 tablespoons Swerve, allulose, or monk fruit

V

In a small mixing bowl combine the water, 1 tablespoon sugar, and yeast, and set aside for 5 minutes until the mixture is frothy.

In a large mixing bowl or the bowl of a stand mixer combine the all-purpose flour, spelt flour, and salt. Add 1 cup of the coconut milk, the melted coconut oil, 3 tablespoons sugar, and the yeast mixture, and stir to combine. Using the dough hook in a stand mixer, knead for about 5 minutes until it forms a smooth ball. Alternately, knead for 15 minutes by hand. Cover with a towel or plastic wrap, and let the dough rise for about an hour, until it has doubled in size.

Grease a 9×13-inch pan with coconut oil. Gently deflate the dough in the bowl with your hands and place it onto a floured work surface. Separate the dough into 12 equal portions, and roll them each into smooth balls. Place the balls in the previously prepared pan, cover with a towel or plastic wrap, and let it rise again for about 45 minutes.

Meanwhile, in a small mixing bowl, combine the remaining 1 cup coconut milk, ¼ cup sugar, and sweetener. Set aside.

Preheat the oven to 350°F.

Pour about two-thirds of the sweetened coconut milk mixture over the buns, then bake for 30 minutes. Remove the pan from the oven and pour the remaining coconut sauce over the top. Serve warm.

Sebastian Ocean Spelt Focaccia

There are many different types of seaweed, and Ariel's friend Sebastian was probably acquainted with many of them, thanks to all of his travel following Ariel around. Mineral-rich kombu is one type of seaweed, and it's a surprisingly common addition to focaccia. That's for good reason: It adds a wonderful flavor known as umami. That makes this otherwise plain bread into its own delectable snack.

Makes 10 servings

2¼ teaspoons (1 package) active dry yeast

1 teaspoon honey

1 cup warm water

2 cups spelt flour, with extra on hand

2 tablespoons kombu flakes

¾ teaspoon salt

1½ tablespoons extra-virgin olive oil, divided

RSF, Veg, LF, WG

In the bowl of a stand mixer, proof the yeast by stirring honey into the warm water and adding the yeast on top. Let sit for 5 to 10 minutes, until the yeast looks foamy. Add the spelt flour and set the mixer to low. As it begins to mix, add the kombu flakes, salt, and 1 tablespoon oil, then increase speed to medium. Mix until the dough becomes smooth, 3 to 5 minutes. To make the dough by hand, combine all the ingredients in a mixing bowl, then knead for 15 minutes. If the dough is too sticky and not forming a ball, add additional flour 1 tablespoon at a time. It may take anywhere from an additional tablespoon to an additional ¼ cup of flour, depending on the weather, age of your flour, and other environmental factors.

Coat a separate mixing bowl with oil. Remove the dough from the mixer and place in the oiled bowl. Cover loosely with a tea towel or oiled plastic wrap, and let rise until doubled in size, about 50 minutes.

Line a baking sheet with parchment paper. Remove the dough from the bowl and place on a floured surface. Punch down gently, and press or roll into a circle or square shape. It should be about ½ inch thick. Place rolled or pressed dough onto the lined baking sheet, and let rise again for 20 minutes. During that time, preheat your oven to 400°F.

After 20 minutes, poke holes gently with your fingers all over the dough, then brush remaining ½ tablespoon oil over the dough. Place it in the oven and bake until golden, about 20 minutes. Let cool before serving.

Lumiere Baguettes

Every good dinner party needs bread to share, and this healthier take on baguettes will be a staple of any "Be Our Guest" party. It's made with a blend of whole wheat, spelt, and white flours. The combination is not only healthier than just using white flour, it also creates the perfect golden color reminiscent of Belle's friend Lumiere.

Makes 2 baguettes

1 tablespoon honey

1¼ cups warm water

2¼ teaspoons (1 package) active dry yeast

1 cup whole wheat flour, with more on hand

2 cups spelt flour

1 cup all-purpose flour

2 teaspoons salt

RSF, V, LF, WG

In the bowl of a stand mixer, combine the honey and warm water and stir to mix. Sprinkle the yeast on top. Let sit for 5 to 10 minutes, until the yeast looks foamy. Add the whole wheat flour, spelt flour, and all-purpose flour, and set the mixer to low.

Add the salt once the flour begins to be incorporated. Increase the mixer speed to medium and mix until the dough is smooth and stretchy, about 10 minutes. To make the dough by hand, combine the ingredients, then knead by hand, about 20 minutes. If the dough is too sticky and not forming a ball, add additional all-purpose flour 1 tablespoon at a time. It may take anywhere from an additional tablespoon to an additional ¼ cup of flour, depending on the weather, age of your flour, and other environmental factors.

Coat a separate mixing bowl with oil. Remove dough from the mixer and place in the oiled bowl. Cover loosely with a tea towel or oiled plastic wrap, and let rise until doubled in size, about 50 minutes.

If you don't have a double baguette pan, line a baking sheet with parchment paper. Remove the dough from the bowl and place on a floured surface. Punch down gently, and divide the dough into two pieces. Roll each half of the dough into a long baguette shape. If you have a double baguette pan, place on the baguette pan once formed. If you don't, place on the lined baking sheet. Slice four or five cuts across the length of each baguette and let rest for 20 minutes.

During that time, preheat the oven to 375°F. Bake bread until golden in color and hollow-sounding when thumped with your hand, about 25 minutes.

CHAPTER 3

Little Hands Appetizers

Mrs. Potts "Gray Stuff" Mini Toasts

Try the gray stuff, it's delicious! There's no need to ask the dishes if this recipe is yummy, either. This version of the gray stuff is a mixed mushroom pâté. It's an appealing and vegetable-rich take on the mystery dish served to Belle as her friends sing "Be Our Guest" around her. When served on whole grain mini toasts and garnished with fresh herbs or microgreens, it's a healthful snack or prelude to a meal, whether you have guests or not.

Makes 6 servings

½ tablespoon extra-virgin olive oil

2 tablespoons finely minced shallot

1 teaspoon minced garlic

1 cup thinly sliced cremini mushrooms

½ cup thinly sliced button mushrooms

½ cup thinly sliced shiitake mushrooms

½ teaspoon dried thyme

2 tablespoons sherry vinegar

¾ teaspoon salt

½ cup toasted walnuts

1 package mini toasts

¼ cup fresh thyme, dill, parsley, or microgreens

RSF, V, LF

Heat the olive oil in a large skillet over medium-high heat. Once hot, add the shallots and sauté for 5 minutes, stirring occasionally. Add the garlic, mushrooms, and dried thyme. reduce the heat to medium, and sauté for 5 minutes, stirring occasionally, until mushrooms begin to release their liquid. Add the sherry vinegar and salt, stir well, and cook for 2 to 3 minutes more, until mushrooms are soft. Let cool.

Combine the mushroom mixture and walnuts in a food processor, and process until nearly smooth, similar in texture to a meat pâté.

To serve, place a scoop on a mini toast, spread to the edges, and top with a sprinkle of herbs or microgreens.

Mulan Tea Eggs

To do her best in battle, Mulan needs snacks that will give her energy and help her brain work quickly. Eggs are high in protein and one of the best dietary sources of choline, an important nutrient for brain power. This exciting version of boiled eggs is made by cracking eggshells before marinating the eggs. If you don't have tamari sauce on hand and can tolerate the gluten in soy sauce, you can substitute an equal amount.

Makes 12 eggs

⅓ cup tamari sauce

1 teaspoon five-
     spice powder

2 teaspoons honey

½ teaspoon salt

2 black tea bags

12 eggs

Salt and black pepper

GF, RSF, Veg, LC

To make the marinade, in a medium-size saucepan combine the tamari, five-spice powder, honey, salt, tea bags, and 2½ cups water. Bring to a boil, then reduce heat and simmer for 10 minutes. Strain and set aside to cool.

To cook the eggs, place the raw eggs in a medium-size pot and cover with water. Bring to a boil, then reduce to a simmer and cook to your desired level of doneness: 7 minutes for soft- to medium-boiled eggs, or 10 minutes for hard-boiled eggs. Remove the eggs from the water and place them in an ice bath to chill quickly. Once chilled, tap the eggs gently all over with the back of a spoon. You want small cracks all over the surface. Don't tap too hard, or you'll create cracks too large for the design to be prominent.

To marinate the eggs, place them in a resealable plastic bag and pour the marinade over them. Seal tightly and marinate in the fridge for 24 hours, turning over after 8 to 12 hours to make sure the marinade permeates all parts of the eggs.

To serve, remove the eggs from the marinade and peel off the cracked shells. The eggs should have a marbled appearance, with dark brown coloring from the marinade. Sprinkle with salt and black pepper, if desired.

Fa Zhou Baked Egg Rolls

While Fa Zhou may not have eaten these with Mulan due to their New York origin in the 1930s, he would surely love this flavor-packed crunchy appetizer. Baking instead of frying cuts way back on oil, and a honey-based sweet-hot dipping sauce keeps refined sugars at bay. These crunchy little delights are quite literally packed with veggies!

Makes 20 egg rolls

- 1 tablespoon plus 1 teaspoon sesame oil, divided
- 3 cloves garlic, minced, divided
- 1 tablespoon plus 1 teaspoon grated fresh ginger, divided
- 3 scallions, thinly sliced
- 1½ cups mushrooms, chopped
- 2 medium carrots, shredded
- 6 cups finely shredded green cabbage, about one small head
- 1 teaspoon cornstarch
- 5 tablespoons soy sauce, divided
- 20 egg roll wrappers
- ¼ cup vegetable oil or cooking spray
- ½ cup honey
- 1 tablespoon rice vinegar
- ½ teaspoon hot sauce, such as sambal oelek, sriracha, or Tabasco

RSF, Veg, LF

To make the egg rolls, heat 1 tablespoon sesame oil over medium heat in a very large skillet or wok. Add 2 cloves of garlic, 1 tablespoon of grated ginger, and the scallions, and sauté until slightly softened and fragrant, about 1 to 2 minutes. Add the mushrooms and continue to sauté 5 minutes. Add the carrots and cook for 1 minute, then add the cabbage. Stir together well and cook until cabbage has reduced by half, about 10 minutes, stirring occasionally.

Dissolve the cornstarch into 4 tablespoons of the soy sauce and add to the cabbage mixture. Stir to coat and remove from the heat, transferring the vegetable mixture to a bowl.

Preheat the oven to 425°F. Prepare a baking sheet by covering it with foil. Place one egg roll wrapper at a time on a clean surface and place about ¼ cup of the cabbage mixture just off-center, close to one of the corners on the square. Roll the corner up and over the filling, fold each side in, and then roll the rest of the way up. Keep a small bowl of water nearby and swipe it across the edges to hold the corners of the egg roll wrapper in place. Repeat with remaining wrappers.

Place the rolls on the baking sheet, covering each roll with oil on all sides by brushing it on or using cooking spray. Bake for 20 minutes, rotating the rolls halfway through cooking.

To make the dipping sauce, in a small mixing bowl combine the honey, rice vinegar, hot sauce, remaining 1 teaspoon garlic, remaining 1 teaspoon ginger, remaining 1 tablespoon soy sauce, and remaining 1 teaspoon sesame oil, and whisk to combine. Taste and adjust seasonings to your liking.

Jaq and Gus Cheese Board

All mice love cheese, but Cinderella's friends Jaq and Gus also love being helpful and gather the materials needed to make Cinderella's beautiful ball gown. Let's learn how to create a gorgeous cheese board full of whole-food nuts and fruits. With a fun focus on ingredients that resemble the elements needed to create a gown, it will be a cheese board that's like an edible version of a night at the ball.

Makes 6 servings

½ cup fruit jam

¼ cup whole grain mustard

3 wedges of cheese: one soft, one medium, and one hard

6 slices prosciutto (to resemble ribbons)

1 cup shelled pistachios (to resemble jade beads)

1 cup dried blueberries (to resemble buttons)

1 cup almonds

1 apple, thinly sliced

1 cup dried apricots

Bread, crackers, or crudités, for serving

RSF

Begin by choosing a large serving platter; it can be a standard wooden board or a serving tray. Place the jam and mustard each in small serving dishes. Place the wedges of cheese on the board, spaced somewhat evenly apart with each one in the center of a third of the board. Place the jam and mustard on the board, one on each side. Arrange the prosciutto on the board in long ribbons. Then drop each of the remaining ingredients by the handful around the board in various spots.

Serve with bread, crackers, or crudités.

Harris, Hubert, and Hamish Smoked Salmon Potato Skins

Merida's little brothers Harris, Hubert, and Hamish stole sweets more than savories, but these potato skins full of Scottish flavors could very well be on their list, too! Baked potato skins are usually loaded with sour cream and bacon, but this version instead has omega-rich smoked salmon and low-fat Greek yogurt. For a presentation that gives an extra nod to the triplets, choose new red potatoes instead of golden ones, in honor of the boys' red hair.

Makes 20 potato skins

10 new red potatoes (about 3 pounds)

2 ounces hot-smoked salmon, chopped

½ cup low-fat plain Greek yogurt

1 tablespoon extra-virgin olive oil

1 teaspoon dried dill

1 tablespoon minced scallions, plus more for garnish, optional

⅛ teaspoon black pepper

1 tablespoon grated Parmesan cheese

½ teaspoon salt, divided

GF, RSF

Preheat oven to 400°F. Line a baking sheet with parchment paper. Prick the potatoes several times with a fork and place on the lined baking sheet. Bake for 45 to 50 minutes, until slightly soft to the touch. Let cool.

In a medium mixing bowl mix the salmon, Greek yogurt, oil, dill, scallions, black pepper, Parmesan cheese, and ¼ teaspoon salt.

Once cooled, slice the potatoes lengthwise in half and scoop out the middles of each. Take care to hold the potatoes tightly so the skins don't break, and to leave at least ¼ inch of flesh around every edge. Set aside two-thirds of the potato flesh for another use. Mash the remaining one-third with a potato masher. Add the mashed potato to the yogurt-and-salmon mix, and fold well to incorporate. Sprinkle the remaining ¼ teaspoon salt over the empty potato skins.

Place a scoop of the mixture into each hollowed-out potato skin and press gently. Set the oven to broil with a rack 6 inches from the heating elements and broil the stuffed potato skins on the baking sheet for 2 to 3 minutes. Sprinkle with additional scallions, if desired.

Flit Berry Pudding Dip

Pocahontas's hummingbird friend Flit is tiny, just like the berries in this pudding dip. And hummingbirds notoriously love sweet things! *Wojapi* is the name for a Native American berry sauce that is thickened into a jam-like texture. Though fresh berries are great, this wojapi recipe is just as good if made with frozen berries instead. If using frozen berries, thaw and drain them before starting this recipe. It has a pudding-like texture, and by serving it with fruit cut into crudités, it could double as a dessert.

Makes 4 servings

2 cups blueberries

1 cup raspberries

1 cup blackberries

2 tablespoons honey, or more to taste

Sliced fruit or crackers, for serving

RSF, Veg, LF

In a medium-size saucepan over low heat, combine the blueberries, raspberries, blackberries, honey, and ½ cup water. Smash the fruit with a spatula or potato masher to release the juices and help it break down.

Cook until the mixture is soft and thickened, about 30 minutes, stirring frequently enough that no bits of fruit stick to the bottom of the pan.

Serve warm or chilled alongside sliced fruit or crackers.

Aladdin Beet Hummus With Roasted Vegetable Chips

This beautiful and colorful chips-and-dip extravaganza is all brought to you by nutritious root vegetables. The gorgeous pink of this hummus evokes the true love Aladdin holds in his heart. The fiber-packed vegetables, lean protein from chickpeas, and heart-healthy olive oil all team up to bring you a whole new world of flavor!

If you have a mandoline, use it to cut the gold beet, zucchini, summer squash, and sweet potato into ⅛-inch-thick slices.

Makes 8 servings

1 medium golden beet, peeled and very thinly sliced

1 zucchini, very thinly sliced

1 yellow summer squash, very thinly sliced

1 medium sweet potato, very thinly sliced

¼ teaspoon salt plus a pinch, divided

½ teaspoon black pepper, divided

1 small red beet, peeled and cut into ½-inch chunks

One 15-ounce can chickpeas, rinsed and drained

Zest and juice from 1 lemon

2 tablespoons tahini

2 cloves garlic

¼ cup olive oil

Toasted sesame seeds and poppy seeds, optional

GF, RSF, V, LF

To make the vegetable chips, preheat the oven to 300°F. Grease or spray a baking sheet with cooking spray. Lay the golden beet, zucchini, summer squash, and sweet potato slices on paper towels and sprinkle with a pinch of salt, then allow to stand for 15 minutes.

Blot any excess moisture from the vegetables with a paper towel, then place them on the prepared baking sheet. Spray cooking spray on the vegetables and sprinkle with ¼ teaspoon of the black pepper. Bake for 30 to 35 minutes, rotating the pan once during baking. Allow to cool a bit before serving.

To make the hummus, steam the red beet chunks for 30 minutes in a vegetable steamer. Let cool, then add the chunks to a food processor with chickpeas, lemon zest and juice, tahini, garlic, olive oil, ¼ teaspoon salt, and the remaining ¼ teaspoon black pepper. Process until completely smooth.

Transfer the hummus to a serving dish and serve alongside the vegetable chips. Sprinkle with sesame seeds and poppy seeds, if desired.

Snow White Forest Toast

Avocado toast is a simple appetizer or snack that's hugely popular because it combines chewy bread and soft, rich avocado. In this recipe, it evokes the feeling of Snow White's forest thanks to the addition of bright microgreens. When you add poppy and sesame seeds on top, you get an even stronger forest feel. Their savory crunch is pretty tasty, too! You won't get lost in this forest, but you will be reminded of Snow White's adventures.

Makes 8 toasts

2 large, thick pieces of whole wheat bread, lightly toasted

1 medium avocado

¼ cup microgreens

1 tablespoon poppy seeds

1 tablespoon sesame seeds

¼ teaspoon salt

Edible flowers, optional

RSF, V, WG

Place the two slices of thick toast on a cutting board. Cut the avocado in half, remove the pit, and scoop the flesh out of the skin. Mash the flesh from each half on each piece of toast, and spread it out until it's in a fairly even layer.

Sprinkle half the microgreens over the avocado on each toast, then sprinkle the poppy and sesame seeds and salt on top. If desired, top with edible flowers.

For younger princesses, cut each toast into four quarters to serve.

CHAPTER 4

Shareable Entrées

Cast-Iron Angel Hair Pie

Does your angel hair pasta get all tangled when you try to eat it? Transform this tangly pasta into a crispy, crunchy pie cooked in Rapunzel's favorite weapon: a cast-iron pan. This pasta dish is flavored with a quick homemade marinara sauce that cooks up in less than a half-hour, plus fresh basil and low-fat mozzarella cheese. It's vegetarian yet plenty filling.

Makes 8 servings

- 1 tablespoon extra-virgin olive oil
- 2 tablespoons minced garlic (3 to 4 cloves)
- 1 tablespoon dried Italian herb blend
- 3½ cups tomato puree
- 2 tablespoons tomato paste
- 1 tablespoon red wine vinegar
- 1 teaspoon honey
- 1 teaspoon salt
- ⅛ teaspoon black pepper
- ½ cup grated Parmesan cheese
- 1 cup plain low-fat Greek yogurt
- 4 eggs
- 12 ounces angel hair pasta, cooked per package instructions
- ⅓ cup lightly packed fresh basil leaves, plus more for garnish
- 8 ounces low-fat fresh mozzarella cheese, sliced

RSF, Veg

To make the marinara sauce, heat the olive oil in a medium saucepan over medium-high heat. Add the garlic and Italian herb mix, and sauté for 1 minute, stirring frequently to ensure the garlic doesn't burn. Add the tomato puree and tomato paste, and sauté for 2 minutes, until the tomato products get slightly darkened. Bring to a boil; add the vinegar, honey, salt, and black pepper, and reduce to a simmer. Simmer for 20 minutes.

To assemble the pie, preheat the oven to 350°F, then prepare your cast-iron skillet. Grease or coat with cooking spray if it's not well-seasoned. In a large mixing bowl combine the Parmesan cheese, yogurt, and eggs, and whisk until smooth. Add the cooked pasta and marinara sauce, and toss to thoroughly coat the pasta.

Pour into the prepared cast-iron skillet and press flat. Stack the basil leaves on top of each other, gently roll them into a cigar shape, then use a sharp knife to slice them into thin ribbons. Top the pasta mixture with the basil then mozzarella. Bake until the mozzarella is golden and melted, about 40 minutes.

Let cool for 5 minutes before serving. Top with additional basil leaves. Cut into wedges as you would a pie.

Tiana Gumbo Rolls

Gumbo is a New Orleans staple, and Tiana loves her New Orleans cuisine! This gumbo is given a makeover with a handheld appeal that makes it fun to eat. The fresh gumbo is scooped into hollowed-out wheat rolls so that it's portable and pleasing to small hands, and also works well for entertaining. A small amount of roux is made for flavor's sake, but the remainder of thickening occurs from potatoes. It may not be the way of eating gumbo that Tiana is most familiar with, but it's so fun that she'd love it anyway!

Makes 12 stuffed rolls

- 4 tablespoons all-purpose flour
- 5 tablespoons neutral oil, divided
- 1 cup diced onion (1 large onion)
- 2 tablespoons Cajun seasoning
- 2 andouille chicken sausages, sliced into ¼-inch coins
- 2 cups diced bell peppers (2 bell peppers)
- 1 cup diced celery (2 to 3 celery stalks)
- 1 cup diced carrots (2 carrots)
- 3½ cups vegetable stock or chicken stock
- ½ pound shrimp, any size
- 1 cup cooked and mashed potato (1 medium potato)
- Salt to taste
- 2 tablespoons minced fresh parsley
- 12 whole wheat rolls

RSF, WG

To make the roux, in a small saucepan over medium-low heat whisk together the flour and 2 tablespoons of the oil. Cook very slowly until the roux is dark brown, about 40 minutes, whisking or stirring frequently. Set aside.

To make the gumbo, heat the remaining 3 tablespoons oil in a large pot over medium-high heat. Add the onion, Cajun seasoning, and sausages, and sauté for 5 minutes. Add the bell peppers, celery, and carrots, and sauté 5 minutes more. Then add the stock and the roux. Bring to a boil, then reduce heat and simmer, covered, until vegetables are barely soft, about 15 minutes. Add the shrimp to the pot, stir to incorporate, and cook, covered, 5 minutes more. Add the mashed potato, then taste for salt. (The amount you need to add will depend on how salty your stock or broth is.) Set aside to cool.

To prepare the rolls, use an apple corer or a knife to cut out the center of each one. Leave enough bread around the edges that the stew won't be able to soak through the edges.

To assemble, generously spoon gumbo into the rolls. (Refrigerate remaining gumbo in an airtight container.)

Note: Traditional gumbo often includes gumbo filé or filé powder, but it can be difficult to find, so we have omitted it from this recipe. If you have sassafras powder on hand, you can add it at the end of the cooking process to give your gumbo a more classic flavor.

Belle Cheese Soufflé

A soufflé is a magical dish, requiring little more than whipped eggs to create a fluffy, tall meal centerpiece. You have to be very careful with it, though, as things like slamming the oven door too hard can lead it to collapse. Everyone will want to be your guest when you turn egg whites into puffy soufflés featuring the French cheeses Belle surely enjoys.

Makes 2 main-dish servings or 4 side-dish servings

- 6 tablespoons unsalted butter, softened, divided
- ¼ cup grated Parmesan cheese
- 3½ tablespoons all-purpose flour
- 1 cup whole milk
- ½ teaspoon salt
- ½ teaspoon black pepper
- 5 cold large egg whites
- ½ teaspoon cream of tartar
- 1 teaspoon Dijon mustard
- 4 large egg yolks
- ¾ cup freshly grated Gruyère or other semifirm French cheese, such as Comté

RSF, Veg

Set an oven rack to lowest position. Preheat the oven to 375°F. Spread 2 tablespoons softened butter around the inside of a large (6-cup) soufflé dish. Add the Parmesan cheese and rotate the dish so cheese sticks to the edges. Place the dish in the refrigerator while continuing with the recipe.

In a small saucepan melt 3 tablespoons butter over medium-high heat until just melted; do not brown. Add the flour and whisk to form a paste. Continue to cook, stirring, until the raw flour scent is gone, about 1 minute. Whisking constantly, add the milk in a thin, steady stream, or in increments of a couple of tablespoons at a time, whisking thoroughly until completely smooth. Switch to a rubber spatula and heat, stirring, until the sauce comes to a simmer. Reduce the heat to low and continue to cook, stirring and scraping the sides and bottom of the pan for 3 minutes. Add the salt and pepper. Transfer to a large heatproof mixing bowl, and allow to cool slightly.

In the bowl of a stand mixer or a large mixing bowl, combine the egg whites and cream of tartar, and beat until firm glossy peaks form. Set aside.

Return to the slightly cooled soufflé base and whisk in mustard. Whisking constantly, add the yolks one at a time. Add one-third of the beaten egg whites, and stir well until the consistency has loosened a bit. Mix in the shredded cheese and gently fold in the remaining egg whites until just combined.

Retrieve the prepared baking dish from the refrigerator and place on a rimmed baking sheet. Transfer the batter to the baking dish and smooth with a spatula.

Bake until fully set, about 35 to 40 minutes, and serve immediately.

Lumiere French Onion Soup du Jour

We may not know exactly what the soup du jour was that Belle enjoyed at the Beast's castle, but since Belle lives in France, French onion soup seems like an appropriate guess. In this recipe, beef broth is replaced with the deep and rich taste of a homemade vegetable broth. It's full of flavorful ingredients such as leeks and shallots, resulting in a vegan take on the classic dish that's so good, you don't even need the typical cheese-and-crouton topping.

Makes 6 servings

For the broth

1 large leek, washed and cut into 1-inch cubes

2 shallots, sliced into ½-inch pieces

2 carrots, sliced into ½-inch coins

4 stalks celery, sliced into ½-inch pieces

8 mushrooms, quartered

5 cloves garlic, quartered

4 roma tomatoes, quartered

3-inch piece kombu, optional

1 bay leaf

½ tablespoon salt, plus more to taste

For the soup

1 tablespoon extra-virgin olive oil

5 large or 6 small sweet onions, thinly sliced

1 tablespoon honey

1 tablespoon flour

⅛ teaspoon black pepper

RSF, V, LF

To make the broth, in a large pot combine the leek, shallots, carrots, celery, mushrooms, garlic, tomatoes, kombu (if using), bay leaf, salt, and 3 quarts water. Bring to a boil, then reduce to a simmer and cook for 1 hour. Let cool slightly, then strain through a fine-mesh strainer into a bowl.

To make the soup, heat the olive oil in a large pot over medium-high heat. Add the onions and toss well to coat with oil. Sauté for 5 minutes. Add the honey, reduce heat to medium low, and continue to sauté, stirring regularly, until the onions are well caramelized, 45 to 50 minutes.

Sprinkle the flour over the onions and stir well for 1 to 2 minutes, until the flour is lightly golden in color. Add ¼ cup of the vegetable broth and stir well to make sure the flour disperses into it. Then add an additional 2 quarts of broth and bring to a simmer. Add black pepper, and taste; you may wish to add additional salt.

Remove the bay leaf and serve hot.

Pocahontas Wild Rice Stuffed Squash

This versatile recipe makes a wonderful vegan main dish and works just as well as a side or appetizer. You can use your choice of squash here, as a variety of squash were staples for Native Americans. Wild rice is a nutrient-dense "pseudo grain" and was considered a valuable staple to many during Pocahontas's time. Pocahontas paints with all the colors of the wind, but you can paint with the colors of your kitchen in this beautifully presented squash.

Makes 4 entrée servings, or 8 side-dish servings

½ cup wild rice, uncooked

1 cup vegetable broth

2 acorn, butternut, or sugar pie pumpkin squash

1 teaspoon salt, divided

1 teaspoon black pepper, divided

3 tablespoons olive oil

1 medium yellow onion, diced

3 ribs celery, diced

1 apple, diced

½ teaspoon dried sage (or 1 tablespoon fresh thyme, finely chopped)

½ teaspoon dried thyme (or 1 tablespoon fresh thyme, finely chopped)

1 tablespoon finely chopped fresh parsley

½ cup chopped hazelnuts

½ cup dried cranberries

2 tablespoons lemon juice (about half a lemon)

GF, RSF, V, LF

Preheat the oven to 400°F. Line a baking sheet with parchment paper.

Combine the wild rice and vegetable broth in a medium pot. Place a lid on the pot and bring the broth to a boil over high heat. Reduce the heat to low, and let the rice simmer for 45 minutes.

Cut each squash in half lengthwise and scoop out the seeds. Season the cut side of each squash with ½ teaspoon each of the salt and black pepper. Place the squash on the prepared baking sheet, cut-side down. Bake for 20 minutes. Set aside.

Heat the oil in a medium skillet; add the onion, and cook over medium heat until soft, about 5 minutes. Add the celery and cook another 2 minutes. Add the apple, sage, thyme, parsley, and remaining ½ teaspoon each of salt and black pepper. Cook for an additional 3 to 5 minutes, until the apple is soft. Add the cooked wild rice, hazelnuts, cranberries, and lemon juice.

Fill the squash cavities with the rice mixture. Bake for 20 to 30 minutes, until the squash is soft and filling is set. Serve hot.

Ariel Nori Veggie Rolls

Seaweed is a healthy staple for any mermaid princess like Ariel. Easy to make and even easier to eat, vegetable nori rolls are an excellent introduction to sushi for kids, as well as a sound choice for people who don't consume raw fish. Consider the fillings here as suggestions, and use your creativity to fill these rolls with thin slices of any vegetables or fruit you and your little princes or princesses love.

Makes 4 rolls

4 cups cooked sushi rice

2 tablespoons rice vinegar

½ tablespoon noncaloric granular sweetener

1 teaspoon salt

4 sheets sushi nori

½ tablespoon sugar

½ cup 1- to 2-inch-long matchstick-cut carrot

½ cup 1- to 2-inch-long matchstick-cut cucumber

1 medium avocado, thinly sliced

GF, Veg, LF

To prep the sushi rice, add the vinegar, sweetener, and salt to the cooked rice and stir well.

To assemble the sushi rolls, place a sheet of nori on a sushi mat or large piece of plastic wrap. Spread one-quarter of the prepared sushi rice onto the mat, using fingers dipped in water to push it close to the edges. You want it to be spread out, but not compressed. Flip it over so that the nori is face-up and rice is face-down. The nori should be horizontal: wider than it is tall.

Near the bottom of the nori, add one-quarter of each filling (carrot, cucumber, avocado) in a thin line horizontally. Fillings should be touching one another with no space between. Starting from the bottom, roll the nori up into a roll, pressing gently as you go. When nearing the end, seal the nori sheet with a couple drops of water from your fingers or a brush, and place it sealed-side down. Repeat with the remaining three rolls.

When all rolls are complete, slice each roll into 8 equal pieces with a wet knife blade to prevent sticking.

Seven Dwarfs Fine Kettle of Fish Stew

In *Snow White and the Seven Dwarfs*, Snow White's friend Grumpy is known for being, well, grumpy—but this delicious fish stew is so good it can change even Grumpy's mood! This stew is similar to a cioppino, with a tomato base and the festiveness of both shellfish and fish fillets; seven types have been chosen in honor of the Seven Dwarfs. The combination, with shells included, makes for a party-worthy presentation.

Makes 8 servings

¼ cup extra-virgin olive oil

3 shallots, finely diced

1 onion, diced

1 fennel bulb, thinly sliced

1 teaspoon salt

1 bell pepper, finely diced

4 garlic cloves, minced

½ teaspoon crushed red pepper flakes

¼ cup tomato paste

One 28-ounce can diced tomatoes in juice

1½ cups dry white wine

4 cups fish stock or chicken stock

One 8-ounce bottle clam juice

2 bay leaves

1 pound manila clams, scrubbed

1 pound mussels, scrubbed and debearded

1 pound shrimp, deveined

½ pound scallops

½ pound cod, deboned and cut into 2-inch chunks

½ pound halibut, deboned and cut into 2-inch chunks

½ pound salmon, deboned and cut into 2-inch chunks

¼ cup fresh parsley, minced

2 lemons, cut into wedges

GF, RSF

In a large saucepan or Dutch oven heat the oil over medium heat. Add the shallots, onion, fennel, and salt; sauté for 5 minutes. Add the bell pepper and sauté another 5 minutes, until softened. Add the garlic and red pepper flakes, and sauté 2 minutes. Stir in the tomato paste. Add the tomatoes with their juice, wine, stock, clam juice, and bay leaves. Cover and let simmer 30 minutes.

Remove the bay leaves. Add the clams and mussels to the pot, and cook for 3 minutes, until some shells open. Add shrimp, scallops, cod, halibut, and salmon. Cover and simmer gently another 5 to 7 minutes, until the remaining shells have opened and seafood is cooked through. (Do not serve any mussels or clams that have not opened.)

To serve, sprinkle a pinch of fresh parsley over each bowl of stew, and serve with a lemon wedge.

Queen Elinor Scottish Stew

Merida's mother, Queen Elinor, is a bit of a traditionalist. She likely enjoys eating lots of the standard Scottish stew, which is a heavy beef dish. However, Queen Elinor also wants Merida to be happy and to teach her new things. This new version of Scottish stew is a great example of moving forward into new ways of life! It's a vegan take on traditional Sottish stew that keeps the signature flavors of tart fruit and tomato. This slow-cooker stew uses jackfruit, which is widely available in cans, to act as a whole-food meat replacement that shreds in a fun, meaty manner.

Makes 6 servings

1 tablespoon extra-virgin olive oil

1 cup diced onion (1 large onion)

1 teaspoon minced garlic

1 tablespoon gluten-free all-purpose flour

1 can jackfruit (2 cups), torn into bite-size pieces

2 cups turnips or rutabagas, cut into ½-inch pieces

1 carrot, sliced into ½-inch coins

½ cup cranberry sauce

1 cup tomato puree

2 cups vegetable broth

1 teaspoon salt

1 teaspoon dried rosemary

¼ teaspoon black pepper

GF, Veg, LF

In a large saucepan heat the olive oil over medium heat. Add the onion and sauté for 2 minutes, just until beginning to turn translucent. Add the garlic and flour, and stir well to coat the onion in flour. Add the jackfruit, turnips or rutabagas, and carrot, and sauté for 5 minutes.

Transfer the ingredients to a slow cooker, and add the cranberry sauce, tomato puree, broth, salt, rosemary, and black pepper. Stir well.

Set the slow cooker to low and cook until the sauce is thickened and the jackfruit and vegetables are tender, about 5 hours. Serve hot.

Prince Phillip Farinata Pizzettes

Chickpea-flour flatbread, also known as *socca* or *farinata*, is a wonderfully nutritious, protein-and-fiber-filled substitute for standard white-flour pizza crusts. The healthy vegetable combo here would surely provide the nourishment Prince Phillip needs to face a dragon! Feel free to swap out the vegetables called for to use up any you have on hand. The crusts go from the hot skillet to a cool baking sheet to keep little hands that might be helping decorate the pizzas safe from burns.

Makes 4 mini pizzas

- ⅔ cup chickpea flour
- ½ teaspoon salt
- ½ teaspoon dried oregano
- ½ teaspoon dried basil
- 3 tablespoons olive oil, divided
- ¼ cup tomato sauce
- ½ cup shredded low-fat mozzarella cheese
- 25 slices black olives
- 10 slices green olives
- 4 slices red bell pepper

GF, RSF, Veg

In a small mixing bowl combine the chickpea flour, ½ cup water, and salt, and whisk until smooth. Cover and allow to sit at room temperature for at least 30 minutes before proceeding (it can be allowed to sit up to overnight).

Preheat the oven to broil, and set a rack 6 inches from the heating element.

Heat a large skillet over medium heat for 4 minutes. Stir the oregano, basil, and 1 tablespoon of the olive oil into the batter. Add the remaining 2 tablespoons oil to the skillet. Pour the batter into four 3-inch circles in the hot pan. Cook for 2 to 3 minutes, and flip with a spatula. Cook for 1 minute, then transfer crusts to a cookie sheet.

Top each crust with 1 tablespoon tomato sauce and 2 tablespoons mozzarella cheese. Arrange the black olives on top of each crust as Phillip's hair, the green olives as his eyes, and the bell pepper pieces as his lips.

Broil 4 to 5 minutes, until cheese is melted and bubbly. Serve hot.

CHAPTER 5

Handheld Treats

Tiana Pecan Praline Bars

Tiana, ever the brilliant chef, creates many famous New Orleans treats in her kitchen. These decadent pecan praline bars use an almond-flour shortbread and a layer of pecans with a luscious maple caramel, providing a generous helping of whole food nutrition! You know anything from Tiana's kitchen has to be mouthwatering perfection, and anything from ours is going to nourish you with plenty of heart-healthy fats and minerals from maple syrup like manganese and zinc. We would wish on the evening star for one (or two) of these bars, please!

Makes 32 bars

For the shortbread

2 cups almond flour

6 tablespoons brown sugar

½ teaspoon salt

2 teaspoons vanilla extract

2½ cups large pecan halves

1 tablespoon pure
    maple syrup

For the caramel

1 cup pure maple syrup

2 tablespoons butter

¼ cup heavy cream

½ teaspoon salt

GF, Veg

Preheat oven to 350°F. Line a 9×13-inch baking pan with foil to cover the bottom and all sides.

To make the shortbread, combine the almond flour, brown sugar, salt, vanilla extract, and maple syrup in a large mixing bowl and stir well until a soft dough forms. Press the dough evenly into the foil-lined pan. Arrange the pecan halves across the top, flat-side down. Set aside while you prepare the caramel.

To make the caramel, heat the maple syrup in a medium saucepan with a heavy bottom. Fit the side with a candy thermometer. Bring the syrup to a boil over medium-high heat until it reaches 225°F to 230°F, just below the soft ball stage. Remove from heat and add the butter, stirring gently until it melts. Add the cream and salt, and mix in gently. Do not stir more than necessary.

Pour the caramel over the shortbread and transfer to the oven. Bake for 25 minutes, or until the caramel begins to solidify around the nuts. Let cool on a wire rack for at least 1 hour, then chill in the refrigerator 1 hour more before slicing and serving.

Pua Purple Yam Tarts

Purple sweet potatoes form the antioxidant-rich filling for these delicious tarts. Moana's friend Pua might be especially fond of these, since the sweet potato is popular on the islands and pigs are good diggers. The vibrant color of the purple sweet potatoes really shines and makes these tarts almost too gorgeous to eat!

Makes 8 tarts

For the tart

2 medium purple sweet potatoes (about 1 pound)

⅔ cup sugar

⅓ cup Swerve, monk fruit, or allulose powder

2 eggs

¾ cup full-fat canned coconut milk

1 teaspoon vanilla extract

1 teaspoon orange extract, optional

¼ teaspoon salt

Finely shredded coconut, for garnish, optional

For the crust

2 cups all-purpose flour

1 tablespoon sugar

½ teaspoon salt

⅓ cup unrefined coconut oil

⅓ cup butter, cubed

3 to 6 tablespoons ice water

Veg

To prepare the sweet potatoes, prick each one several times with a fork and microwave on high for 10 minutes until very soft, flipping once halfway through. Once potatoes are cooked, allow them to cool until they are cool enough to handle.

Meanwhile, prepare the crust. In the bowl of a food processor combine the flour, sugar, salt, coconut oil, and butter, and pulse until coarse crumbs form. Add the ice water, 1 tablespoon at a time, pulsing until a ball forms, making sure to not add more water once the dough sticks together. Chill the dough for 30 minutes.

Preheat the oven to 425°F. Remove the dough from refrigerator, divide in half, and roll out each half on parchment paper, adding flour if needed to prevent sticking. Cut the dough into 5-inch circles using a lid or ring mold as a guide to yield eight circles, and place each circle of dough inside one cavity of a standard muffin tin. Bake the tart shells for 4 minutes, then allow to cool while you prepare the filling.

To assemble the tarts, remove and discard skins from the sweet potatoes. Put the sweet potato flesh in a food processor and blend until smooth. Add the sugar, sweetener, eggs, coconut milk, vanilla extract, orange extract (if using), and salt; blend until smooth. Pour into the partially baked tart shells.

Reduce the oven temperature to 375°F. Bake the tarts for 25 to 30 minutes, or until the filling is solid. Allow them to cool for 30 minutes before removing from the muffin tin. If desired, sprinkle with the shredded coconut.

Snow White Baked Apples

Snow White simply can't resist apples, whether she's baking delicious apple pies for the Seven Dwarfs or taking the dangerous bite from an apple that lulled her off to endless sleep. These perfectly baked apples with a crumbly oat filling just might lull you off to sleep, but we assure you, you'll wake the next morning without the need for a True Love's Kiss.

Makes 4 apples

4 large Granny Smith apples

¾ cup oats

¼ cup chopped walnuts

¼ cup pure maple syrup

¼ cup brown sugar

2 tablespoons butter, softened

1 teaspoon cinnamon

½ teaspoon salt

GF, Veg

Preheat the oven to 350°F.

Using an apple corer or a paring knife, remove the center core of the apples, about three-quarters of the way down, leaving the bottom ½ inch intact. If using a paring knife, cut a circle and then use a small spoon to scoop out the seeds. If the apples won't stand straight, cut off a slice on the bottom so they are flat.

In a small mixing bowl combine the oats, walnuts, maple syrup, brown sugar, butter, cinnamon, and salt, and mix with a fork until the butter is well distributed and the mixture is crumbly. Stuff the mixture evenly into the apple cavities.

Place the apples in a small baking dish and pour boiling water into the bottom of the dish, about ½ inch. Bake 30 to 45 minutes or until the apples are soft, but not mushy and the oat mixture is golden brown. Let cool, but serve warm.

Moana Fruit Pudding

This Tahitian treat, known as po'e, is a traditional island dessert. Incredibly simple to make, and healthy to boot, it's a wonderful way to use up very ripe bananas. This pudding can be eaten by hand or in a bowl topped with luscious coconut cream. If you have an adventurous spirit like Moana, you could try this recipe using a different fruit puree. Just be sure you have 4 cups of it, and the recipe will work the same way.

Makes 6 servings

6 to 8 ripe bananas

⅓ cup brown sugar

3 tablespoons Swerve, allulose, or monk fruit

1 cup cornstarch

2 teaspoons vanilla extract

Pinch of salt

GF, V, LF

Preheat oven to 375°F. In a food processor puree the ripe bananas. Measure out 4 cups, discarding any remaining puree. Add the 4 cups of puree back to the food processor. Add the brown sugar, sweetener, cornstarch, vanilla extract, and salt, and process until the mixture is smooth with no lumps.

Grease or spray a 2-quart baking dish with cooking spray. Pour the puree into the prepared baking dish and bake for 30 to 45 minutes, until the pudding is firm and bubbling.

Allow it to cool for 30 minutes, then cover with plastic and chill in refrigerator until firm, about 2 hours. Cut into squares to serve.

Cinderella Glass Slipper Cookies

Everyone loves a good shortbread cookie, so we have whipped up a deceptively easy base for these decorated cookies with nutrient-dense almond flour. You'll need a slipper-shaped cookie cutter to make these properly resemble Cinderella's glass slipper. You can decorate them as simply or elaborately as you like; some suggestions are included, but feel free to let your imagination take you further. You won't want to leave these cookies behind like Cinderella left her glass slipper on the palace steps!

Makes 15 cookies

For the cookies

½ cup butter, softened

⅓ cup confectioners' sugar

3 tablespoons confectioners' Swerve, allulose, or monk fruit

1 tablespoon vanilla extract

3 cups almond flour

½ teaspoon salt

For the icing

1 cup confectioners' sugar

⅓ cup confectioners' Swerve, allulose, or monk fruit

1 tablespoon honey

1 tablespoon milk, plus 1 tablespoon if needed

1 teaspoon vanilla extract

Blue sugar crystals or other sprinkles, optional

GF, Veg

To make the shortbread, cream together the butter, confectioners' sugar, sweetener, and vanilla extract until creamy. Add the almond flour and salt, and mix until well combined. Form the dough into a square, wrap with plastic, and chill in the refrigerator for 20 to 30 minutes.

Preheat the oven to 325°F. Line a baking sheet with parchment paper.

Place the dough between two sheets of parchment paper and roll until it's about ½ inch thick. Using your cookie cutter, cut the dough into slippers and transfer to the prepared baking sheet.

Bake for 10 to 12 minutes, to a very light golden brown. Allow to cool completely on baking sheet before icing, at least 60 minutes.

To make the icing, combine the confectioners' sugar, sweetener, honey, 1 tablespoon milk, and the vanilla. Add more milk if needed to reach desired consistency.

Spread the frosting on cookies with a knife, or add icing to piping bottles or bags and squeeze onto cookies. If using sugar crystals or sprinkles, add while icing is still wet.

Ariel Seashell Madeleines

These flavorful cookies are deceptively simple to make, thanks to the beautifully shaped madeleine pan. Butter is swapped for heart-healthy olive oil, making for a treat that benefits the body as much as it does your taste buds. The shell shape of these cookies beautifully matches Ariel's under-the-sea outfit, as well as creating a perfectly textured edge to these sweet and simple madeleines.

Makes 18 to 20 cookies

2 large eggs, at room temperature

½ cup honey

¼ cup Swerve, allulose, or monk fruit

2 teaspoons lemon zest, from 1 lemon

2 teaspoons vanilla extract

⅔ cup all-purpose flour

⅓ cup almond flour

½ teaspoon baking powder

⅛ teaspoon salt

½ cup light olive oil

Additional olive oil and flour, for madeleine pan

Confectioners' sugar for dusting, optional

RSF, Veg

Combine the eggs, honey, and sweetener in the bowl of a stand mixer, or a medium mixing bowl. Beat on high until the mixture is fluffy and light in color, about 2 to 3 minutes. Mix in the lemon zest and vanilla extract.

In a small mixing bowl combine the flour, almond flour, baking powder, and salt. Fold into the egg mixture using a spatula, half at a time. Fold in the olive oil. Cover and chill for 30 to 60 minutes.

With about 10 minutes of chilling time left, preheat the oven to 350°F. Grease a madeleine pan using olive oil and a pastry brush, and sprinkle with flour. Remove the batter from the refrigerator, and drop by heaping tablespoons into the prepared pan.

Bake for 10 to 12 minutes or until the tops spring back when lightly pressed with your finger.

Transfer immediately to a wire rack to cool slightly. Dust with confectioners' sugar before serving, if desired.

Flora, Fauna, and Merryweather Meringues

Flora, Fauna, and Merryweather each brought thoughtful gifts to Aurora, and these beautiful reduced-sugar meringues in their classic colors make wonderful gifts, too. While Fauna struggled to make a layered cake, you won't struggle to make these meringues in the fairies' classic colors of red, green, and blue. Be sure not to get any yolks in your whites and use a completely clean and dry mixing bowl for best results.

Makes 80 meringues

4 large egg whites

½ teaspoon cream of tartar

⅔ cup sugar

⅛ teaspoon salt

⅓ cup Swerve, allulose, or monk fruit

1 teaspoon vanilla extract

Natural food coloring in red, green, and blue

GF, Veg, LF

Preheat the oven to 200°F. Line two baking sheets with parchment paper. Combine the egg whites and cream of tartar in the bowl of a stand mixer or a large mixing bowl, and beat until soft peaks form, about 2 minutes in a stand mixer or 10 minutes by hand.

Combine the sugar, salt, and sweetener in a small mixing bowl and stir to combine. Begin to add the sugar mixture to the egg whites, one spoonful at a time, with the mixer still running. Once all the sugar mixture is added, continue to beat the mixture on high until the egg whites are very thick and glossy, and stiff peaks form. Stop the mixer and add the vanilla extract, mixing it in briefly.

Separate the mixture into three bowls and add the coloring, one per bowl, folding in one drop at a time to achieve desired color. Transfer the mixture to a piping bag, and pipe onto prepared baking sheets in 1-inch kisses. They will not spread, so they may be piped close together.

Bake for 60 minutes, then turn off the oven and leave the meringues in the oven with the door closed for an additional hour. Remove from the oven and allow to cool to room temperature before removing from the parchment.

Mushu Sesame Cookie Sandwiches

These sandwich cookies are the perfect size for Mushu—travel size! Mushu would definitely enjoy these crispy sesame-egg white cookies, sandwiched with a sweet and sticky date paste because they would give him lots of energy for long journeys. They will for you too, with the wonderful long-lasting protein of egg whites and mineral-rich dates.

Makes 24 sandwich cookies

For the cookies

½ cup all-purpose flour

2 tablespoons almond flour

5 tablespoons unrefined coconut oil, melted

2 teaspoons toasted sesame oil

Pinch of salt

2 egg whites

¼ cup sugar

2 tablespoons Swerve, allulose, or monk fruit

2 tablespoons sesame seeds

For the filling

1½ cups Medjool dates, pitted and stemmed

Veg, LF

To make the cookies, preheat the oven to 325°F. Line two baking sheets with parchment paper.

In a large mixing bowl combine the all-purpose flour, almond flour, coconut oil, sesame oil, and salt. Combine with a whisk until smooth, but do not overmix.

In the bowl of a stand mixer or in a large mixing bowl, beat egg whites until soft peaks form. Add the sugar and sweetener, one spoonful at a time, beating constantly. Continue to beat until stiff peaks form.

Fold the egg whites into the flour mixture. Transfer the mixture to a piping bag. Pipe 1-inch circles onto the prepared baking sheets. Sprinkle the cookies with sesame seeds. Bake for 15 minutes, until the cookies are a light golden brown. Allow the cookies to cool completely on baking sheets.

To make the filling, place the dates in a small mixing bowl. Boil 3 cups water and pour over the dates, allowing them to soak for 10 minutes. Transfer the dates to a food processor or high-speed blender with ½ cup of the soaking liquid. Blend until completely smooth, adding more soaking liquid if necessary. Transfer the mixture to a small container, and place in the refrigerator until ready to assemble the sandwiches.

To assemble the sandwiches, spread 1 tablespoon date paste on the flat side of one cookie, pressing a second cookie onto it to create a sandwich. Repeat with remaining cookies and filling.

CHAPTER 6

Dessert Shareables

Flynn Lemon Polenta Cake

This recipe provides protein from almond flour, heart-healthy fat from olive oil, and whole grain goodness from polenta. An elegant, gluten-free treat, this cake is shockingly simple to make, and is even better the second day—if it lasts that long! The beautiful yellow perfectly matches the crown of Flynn's desire and the gold of Rapunzel's glowing hair. The grind of your polenta will affect the texture of the cake. Because a bit of texture is enjoyable, medium grind is used here.

Makes 1 cake

For the cake

1 cup almond flour

1 cup medium-grind polenta

1½ teaspoons baking powder

½ teaspoon salt

3 eggs, room temperature

⅔ cup sugar

⅓ cup Swerve, allulose or monk fruit

⅔ cup light olive oil

2 tablespoons lemon juice (about half a lemon)

1 tablespoon lemon zest (from 1 lemon)

1 lemon, very thinly sliced (optional)

For the syrup

¼ cup lemon juice (about 1 lemon)

⅔ cup confectioners' sugar

⅓ cup confectioners' Swerve or monk fruit

GF, Veg, WG

To make the cake, preheat the oven to 350°F. Grease a springform pan and line it with parchment paper. In a medium mixing bowl combine the almond flour, polenta, baking powder, and salt, and whisk together. Set aside.

In a large mixing bowl combine the eggs, sugar, and sweetener, and beat with an electric mixer or whisk until light in color, about 2 minutes. Add the olive oil, lemon juice, and lemon zest, and mix lightly to combine. Gently fold in the dry ingredients with a rubber spatula. Pour the batter into the prepared springform pan, and bake until the cake is golden brown and begins to pull apart from the sides of the pan, about 40 minutes. If the cake begins to brown too soon, cover it with foil. Leave the cake in the pan to cool completely, at least 60 minutes. Remove the cake from the pan. Top the cake with the lemon slices, if desired.

To make the syrup, in a small saucepan combine lemon juice, confectioners' sugar, and sweetener. Bring to a boil and stir until sugar is dissolved, then remove from heat. Prick holes all over the top of the cake (a wooden skewer works well for this) and pour the syrup over it.

Triplets Enchanted Dundee Cake

This beautiful Scottish fruitcake is made healthy and gluten free with almond flour and delicious dried cherries. It's no surprise Merida's little brothers just couldn't resist a cake as perfectly scrumptious as this one. But don't worry! As magical as this cake may be, it won't turn you or anyone in your family into bears!

Makes 8 servings

4 large eggs

½ cup honey

3 tablespoons orange marmalade

1 teaspoon vanilla extract

1 teaspoon pumpkin pie spice

1½ cups almond flour

¼ teaspoon salt

½ teaspoon baking soda

2 tablespoons milk

½ cup dried cherries

½ cup whole blanched almonds, for decorating

GF, Veg, RSF

Preheat the oven to 350°F. Grease or spray an 8-inch round cake pan with cooking spray.

In a large mixing bowl whisk the eggs. One by one, gradually whisk in the honey, marmalade, vanilla extract, pumpkin pie spice, almond flour, salt, and baking soda. Stir in the milk and dried cherries. Transfer to the prepared cake pan. Arrange the blanched almonds on top in a circular pattern.

Bake for 40 minutes or until the cake is firm and a toothpick comes out clean.

Allow to cool for 30 minutes before serving.

Mama Odie Bread Pudding

This recipe combines whole grain bread, protein-rich Greek yogurt and eggs, and sweet apples to create an unforgettable bread pudding! Tiana's friend Mama Odie knows exactly what you need, so get to making this delicious dessert and have some leftovers for breakfast. If you prefer to substitute a different fruit, such as peaches, bananas, or berries, we recommend mixing it in after soaking, with the walnuts.

Makes 12 servings

6 eggs

1 cup low-fat vanilla Greek yogurt

1¼ cups whole milk

¾ cup pure maple syrup

1 tablespoon vanilla extract

2 teaspoons cinnamon

¾ teaspoon salt

1 pound loaf whole grain bread, crusts removed and cubed

4 apples, such as Granny Smith, peeled and chopped in ½-inch chunks

½ cup chopped walnuts

1 tablespoon coconut sugar

Additional Greek yogurt and maple syrup, for serving

RSF, Veg, LF, WG

In a large mixing bowl combine the eggs, yogurt, milk, maple syrup, vanilla extract, cinnamon, and salt, and whisk to combine. Mix in the bread and apples. Cover and refrigerate 4 to 8 hours or overnight.

Preheat the oven to 350°F. Grease a 9×13-inch baking dish. Remove the bread mixture from the fridge and stir in the walnuts. Transfer the mixture to the prepared baking dish. Spray a piece of aluminum foil with cooking spray and cover the pan tightly, spray side down. Bake for 45 minutes, until steaming hot and puffed in the center. Remove the foil and sprinkle with coconut sugar.

Bake, uncovered, for 20 minutes more, until the top is browned. Remove from the oven and allow to cool for 15 to 20 minutes before serving.

Serve with additional yogurt and maple syrup.

Mulan Black Sesame Layered Custard Tart

Warrior Mulan may not have time to do much baking, but surely she enjoys eating these tarts with beautiful black sesame seeds! Traditional egg custard is lightened with almond milk for a dairy-free treat. Whole eggs instead of just yolks provide extra protein, and a layer of black sesame seeds above the vibrant yellow custard adds nutrients and richness.

Makes 10 tarts

For the crusts

2 cups all-purpose flour

1 tablespoon sugar

½ teaspoon salt

⅔ cup unrefined coconut oil

3 to 6 tablespoons ice water

For the filling

¼ cup black sesame seeds

1½ cups almond milk

¼ cup honey

3 whole eggs

1 teaspoon vanilla extract

Pinch of salt

Pinch of turmeric

50 almond slices (optional)

Veg, LF

To make the crusts, in the bowl of a food processor combine the flour, sugar, salt, and coconut oil, and pulse until coarse crumbs are formed. Add ice water 1 tablespoon at a time and pulse until a ball forms, making sure to not add any more water once the dough sticks together. Chill the dough for 30 minutes.

Preheat the oven to 425°F. Divide the dough in half, and roll out each half on parchment paper, adding flour if needed to prevent sticking. Cut the dough into 5-inch circles using a lid or ring mold as a guide to yield 10 circles, and place each circle of dough inside one cup of a standard muffin tin. Chill tart shells in refrigerator while you prepare your filling.

To make the filling, toast the sesame seeds in a small frying pan over medium heat for 2 minutes, stirring constantly. Allow them to cool for 10 minutes, then grind into a powder in a spice grinder or food processor. Set aside.

Pour the almond milk and honey into a medium saucepan, and cook on medium heat until bubbles just begin to form, about 5 minutes. Meanwhile, whisk the eggs in a large mixing bowl. When the almond milk mixture is heated, stream it slowly into the egg mixture, a few tablespoons at a time at first, whisking as you pour. Pour the mixture through a fine-mesh sieve into a container with a pouring lip to remove any bits of egg that may have scrambled. Whisk in the vanilla extract, salt, and turmeric.

Remove the tart shells from the refrigerator and pour the mixture evenly among the shells. Sprinkle the top of each tart with the ground sesame seeds. Bake the tarts for 25 minutes, reducing the heat to 350°F and rotating the pan after 15 minutes. Cool at least 60 minutes before removing tart shells from the pan. Tarts will hold together best after chilling in the refrigerator overnight. Top each tart with five almond slices to resemble a flower, if desired.

Jasmine Date and Walnut Pie

Dates and walnuts are wonderfully nutritious ingredients that likely grow plentifully in Agrabah. This pie inspired by Jasmine does away with corn syrup and shortening, and uses natural and mineral-rich maple syrup and coconut oil instead. This pie is perfect for a picnic on a magic carpet.

Makes 8 to 10 servings

For the crust

1¼ cups all-purpose flour

2 teaspoons sugar

¼ teaspoon salt

⅓ cup unrefined coconut oil

2 to 4 tablespoons ice water

For the filling

⅓ cup brown sugar

3 tablespoons granulated Swerve, allulose, or monk fruit

2 tablespoons melted unrefined coconut oil

1 tablespoon all-purpose flour

¼ teaspoon salt

2 eggs

1 cup pure maple syrup

1¼ cups chopped walnuts

1 cup chopped pitted dates

Veg

To make the crust, combine the flour, sugar, salt, and coconut oil in a food processor and pulse until coarse crumbs form. Add ice water 1 tablespoon at a time and pulse until a ball forms, making sure to not add more water once the dough sticks together. Chill the dough for 30 minutes in the refrigerator.

Preheat the oven to 350°F. Roll the dough out to a 12-inch circle, and press into a greased or sprayed 9-inch pie pan. Flute or crimp the edges by using your fingers to create a wavy shape as they press into the edges of the dough. Return the shell to the refrigerator to chill for an additional 20 minutes.

Once chilled, cover the dough with parchment paper, and fill with two packages of pie weights or dried beans. Bake the crust for 15 minutes. Remove pie from the oven and carefully lift the parchment paper with the weights out of the pie.

To make the filling, in a large mixing bowl whisk together the brown sugar, sweetener, coconut oil, flour, and salt. Whisk in the eggs and maple syrup. Stir in the walnuts and dates. Pour the mixture into the crust and transfer to the oven.

Bake for 40 to 50 minutes. After 20 minutes, cover with a pie crust shield or wrap the edges with foil to prevent heavy browning. Remove the pie from the oven and allow to cool completely before serving, at least 2 hours or overnight.

Aladdin Agrabah Love Cake

Aladdin and Jasmine's love is beautifully represented by this delicate rose water, saffron, and cardamom cake. Designed to be shared with loved ones, this cake is also naturally nutritious, with almond flour, yogurt, and egg packing in plenty of protein. If you can't find culinary-grade rose petals, you can just decorate with pistachios. Either way, it will be delicious and enchanting!

Makes 1 cake

For the cake

6 tablespoons butter, softened

6 tablespoons light olive oil

⅔ cup sugar

⅓ cup Swerve, allulose, or monk fruit

5 large eggs

1 cup low-fat Greek yogurt

2 tablespoons rose water

2 teaspoons ground cardamom

2¼ cups blanched almond flour

2 teaspoons baking powder

Pinch of salt

For the syrup

⅓ cup orange juice

½ cup honey

1 tablespoon rose water

2 tablespoons shelled and crushed pistachios

2 tablespoons fresh or dried edible rose petals, optional

GF, Veg

To make the cake, preheat the oven to 350°F. Grease a 10-inch springform pan and line the bottom with parchment paper. In a large mixing bowl combine the butter, oil, sugar, and sweetener, and whisk together until creamy, about 1 minute. Add the eggs one at a time, whisking after each one. Whisk in the yogurt and beat until mixture is fluffy. Using a spatula, stir in the rose water and cardamom. Add the almond flour, baking powder, and salt, and fold to combine. Pour into the prepared cake pan. Bake for 30 to 40 minutes, until a toothpick comes out clean. Allow the cake to cool for 10 minutes.

To make the syrup, heat the orange juice and honey in a medium saucepan over medium heat until it reaches a boil. Lower the heat to medium-low and let it simmer for 5 minutes. Remove from the heat and stir in the rose water.

Once cool, use a wooden skewer to prick holes all over the cake, an inch or so apart. Pour the syrup over the cake. Allow it to cool an hour or so longer, then decorate the top with pistachios and rose petals (if using).

Cogsworth Lemon Ice Cream

This simple vegan recipe has a surprise ingredient for unbeatable creaminess: avocado! The lemon flavor is prominent in this creamy, simple-to-make ice cream with a vibrant yellow hue that matches Belle's iconic dress. Cogsworth has a sour disposition, but he's sweet underneath—just like this lemon ice cream!

Makes 8 servings

Flesh of 2 medium avocados

One 14-ounce can coconut cream

One 14-ounce can coconut milk

½ cup sugar

¼ cup Swerve, allulose, or monk fruit

1 tablespoon lemon zest (1 lemon)

½ cup lemon juice (2 lemons)

¼ teaspoon salt

Pinch of turmeric

Fresh mint (optional)

GF, V

In a blender combine the avocado, coconut cream, coconut milk, sugar, sweetener, lemon zest and juice, salt, and turmeric. Blend until smooth, about 1 minute, making sure there are no chunks of avocado remaining.

Pour the mixture into your ice cream maker and churn according to manufacturer's instructions, anywhere from 20 to 45 minutes.

When the ice cream has achieved soft-serve texture, remove it from the maker. Serve in bowls with fresh mint, if desired. Or store in a freezer-safe container for 2 hours to firm up further.

Rapunzel Berry Crumble

Berries are one of the most nutritious types of fruit, packed with antioxidants and fiber. Inspired by the yellow-and-pink cupcake Rapunzel and Flynn enjoy, the golden crumble topping here covers the luscious pink and purple berries for a warm and comforting dessert that makes a wonderful breakfast the next morning! Four types of berries combine in this crumble for taste variety, but the recipe is flexible if you can't get them all. You can also use frozen berries if fresh are out of season; just thaw and drain before preparing the recipe.

Makes 8 servings

For the crumble

1 cup gluten-free rolled oats

½ cup brown rice flour

½ cup coconut sugar

½ teaspoon ground cinnamon

¼ teaspoon salt

¼ cup pure maple syrup

½ cup unrefined coconut oil

For the filling

2 cups raspberries

2 cups blueberries

1 cup blackberries

1 cup hulled and quartered strawberries

¼ cup coconut sugar

¼ teaspoon salt

2 tablespoons cornstarch

GF, RSF, V, WG

To make the crumble, preheat the oven to 375°F. Grease or spray an 11×7-inch baking pan with cooking spray.

In a medium mixing bowl combine the oats, brown rice flour, coconut sugar, cinnamon, and salt. Whisk to incorporate, then stir in maple syrup. Add the coconut oil, and using a pastry cutter or fork, cut together until the mixture forms crumbs. Transfer the crumble mixture to the refrigerator while you prepare the filling.

To make the filling, combine the raspberries, blueberries, blackberries, and strawberries in a large mixing bowl. Sprinkle the coconut sugar, salt, and cornstarch over them and gently toss to combine. Transfer the berry mixture to the prepared baking pan and top with the crumble mixture.

Bake until the top is browned and filling is bubbly, 30 to 35 minutes. Serve warm.

CHAPTER 7

Sippables

Abu Watermelon Sparkler

This is a drink that Aladdin's friend Abu would surely want to get his hands on! And even though he's not a big fan of sharing food, this sparkler is so good that Abut would want to share it with Aladdin! Watermelon is such a wonderfully sweet fruit that you can make a sparkling drink of it with no additional sweetener needed. Because you'll be blending the whole fruit into the beverage, you won't lose any of its healthful fiber, either. This sparkler is refreshing on a summer day, but can bring summer vibes into any season if fresh watermelon is available near you.

If you don't have crushed ice on hand, place several ice cubes in a freezer-strength resealable plastic bag, and use a rolling pin or meat mallet to smash the ice into small pieces.

Makes 4 drinks

4 cups cubed fresh watermelon, seeds removed if not seedless

½ teaspoon ground ginger

1 tablespoon lime juice

4 cups crushed ice

Sparkling water

Lime wedge or wheel, for garnish, optional

Slice of watermelon, for garnish, optional

GF, RSF, V, LF

In a blender combine the watermelon, ginger, and lime juice, and blend on high until the mixture looks very smooth.

Pour the watermelon juice into four large glasses. Add crushed ice to the glasses and stir briefly. Top with sparkling water.

If desired, garnish with a lime wedge, lime wheel, or slice of watermelon.

Island Fruit Punch

You don't need a sailing adventure like Moana's to enjoy this punch. Electrolyte-rich coconut water makes for a sweet base, and pineapple and mango add some tang. A swirl of magenta dragon fruit puree creates a beautiful, bright, and colorful presentation. Because fresh dragon fruit can be difficult to find, we use a frozen puree for convenience.

Makes 6 drinks

One 32-ounce container coconut water

1 cup pineapple juice

1 cup mango nectar

1 cup orange juice

1½ cups chopped fresh mango pieces

Ice

½ cup frozen dragon fruit puree, thawed and thinned with ½ cup water

6 thin slices pineapple

GF, RSF, V, LF

Pour the coconut water, pineapple juice, mango nectar, orange juice, and mango pieces into a serving bowl or pitcher. Stir well to combine.

Fill six glasses with ice. Pour the punch mixture into each glass until three-quarters full, making sure to get some mango pieces in each.

Pour about 2½ tablespoons dragon fruit puree into each glass, and let it settle throughout the glasses.

Add a pineapple slice to each glass before serving.

Cinderella Latte

To make this Cinderella-inspired latte, you need both pumpkin puree and pumpkin pie spice. With the combination of these delicious flavors, Cinderella would surely have wanted to stay at the ball past midnight! Substitute decaf espresso for little ones or evening enjoyment.

Makes 1 drink

1 cup milk, divided

2 tablespoons white chocolate chips

1 teaspoon pumpkin puree

¼ teaspoon pumpkin pie spice, plus more for serving

1 teaspoon honey

2 ounces brewed espresso

GF, Veg, LF

In a small saucepan heat ½ cup of the milk with the white chocolate chips, pumpkin puree, pumpkin pie spice, honey, and espresso over low heat until the chips have melted and the mixture is very warm.

In a separate saucepan or cup froth the remaining ½ cup milk with a milk frother until a tight foam has formed.

Pour the latte into a mug and scoop foam on top. Sprinkle with additional pumpkin pie spice.

Aurora Chamomile Slushie

Bedtime is rarely the most fun time of day for young princesses, even for Aurora. Sleepytime can be made more fun with a cup of tea, and when that tea is a slushie it's practically a festive occasion! Calming chamomile tea is premade and chilled as the base for this slushie so you don't have to worry about it melting the ice. Cherries and honey are also known for promoting good sleep.

Makes 2 slushies

1½ cups chilled brewed chamomile tea

⅓ cup tart cherry juice

2 teaspoons honey

Stevia to taste

1½ cups ice cubes

GF, RSF, V, LF

In a blender combine the tea, cherry juice, honey, stevia, and ice. Blend on high speed just until the ice is slushie texture.

Pour into two glasses to serve.

Snow White Chocolate

You might not believe that a vegan white chocolate drink could be as comforting and creamy as a dairy one, but this one surely is! Freshly made cashew milk is used for both its nutrition and its richness, and chocolate extract provides deep chocolate flavor without much color. This drink is indeed the fairest of them all, and it's excellent hot or iced.

Makes 4 drinks

1 cup raw cashews

1 teaspoon
    chocolate extract

1 teaspoon vanilla extract

1 tablespoon sugar

Stevia to taste

Pinch of salt

GF, RSF, V, LC

Soak the cashews in 2 cups water for at least 1 hour or up to 8 hours.

Drain and rinse the cashews. Add the cashews to a blender with 2 cups fresh water, the chocolate extract, vanilla extract, sugar, stevia, and salt.

Blend on high until you can't see any little pieces of cashew.

Strain into a bowl through a nut milk bag or multiple layers of cheesecloth, squeezing out all the liquid. Make sure to not squeeze too hard, or bits of cashew might come through the bag or cloth.

For a hot beverage, heat the drink in a saucepan over medium-low heat until very warm, then pour into mugs.

For an iced beverage, pour 1 cup of the drink into glasses filled with ice.

King Triton Ocean Fizz

This drink looks like an ocean in a glass, but it's much better tasting than that. It uses fresh mint, lime, and blueberries as the key ingredients to give it the colors found in the sea. If King Triton were looking for a drink to remind him of home, this could be at the top of his list! The delicious flavor is reminiscent of a mojito. For the lemon-lime soda, a stevia-sweetened sugar-free option is the most healthful choice.

Makes 4 drinks

1 cup blueberries, fresh or thawed if frozen

2 tablespoons lime juice

4 sprigs of fresh mint, plus 12 mint leaves

4 lime wedges

Ice

2 cans lemon-lime soda

4 lime wedges, for garnish

4 sprigs of mint, for garnish

RSF, GF, V, LF

In a large cup or a cocktail shaker muddle the blueberries, lime juice, and mint leaves together until the blueberries are fully smashed and mint leaves are broken down into small pieces.

Pour one-fourth of the mixture into each of four tall glasses, then fill glasses with ice. Stir briefly.

Fill glasses with soda and garnish each drink with a lime wedge and a mint sprig.

Index

INSIGHT
EDITIONS

PO Box 3088
San Rafael, CA 94912
www.insighteditions.com

f Find us on Facebook: www.facebook.com/InsightEditions
𝕏 Follow us on Twitter: @insighteditions

Disnep

Library of Congress Cataloging-in-Publication Data available.

ISBN: 978-1-64722-376-2

INSIGHT EDITIONS
Publisher: Raoul Goff
VP of Licensing and Partnerships: Vanessa Lopez
VP of Creative: Chrissy Kwasnik
VP of Manufacturing: Alix Nicholaeff
Editorial Director: Vicki Jaeger
Editor: Anna Wostenberg
Production Editor: Jennifer Bentham
Production Manager: Greg Steffen
Senior Production Manager, Subsidiary Rights: Lina s Palma

WATERBURY PUBLICATIONS, INC.
Editorial Director: Lisa Kingsley
Creative Director: Ken Carlson
Associate Editor: Tricia Bergman
Associate Editor: Maggie Glisan
Associate Art Director: Doug Samuelson
Production Assistant: Mindy Samuelson
Photographer: Ken Carlson
Food Stylist: Jennifer Peterson
Food Stylist Assistant: Catherine Fitzpatrick

 ROOTS of PEACE ⊕ REPLANTED PAPER

Insight Editions, in association with Roots of Peace, will plant two
trees for each tree used in the manufacturing of this book. Roots
of Peace is an internationally renowned humanitarian organization
dedicated to eradicating land mines worldwide and converting
war-torn lands into productive farms and wildlife habitats. Roots
of Peace will plant two million fruit and nut trees in Afghanistan
and provide farmers there with the skills and support necessary for
sustainable land use.

Manufactured in China by Insight Editions

10 9 8 7 6 5 4 3 2

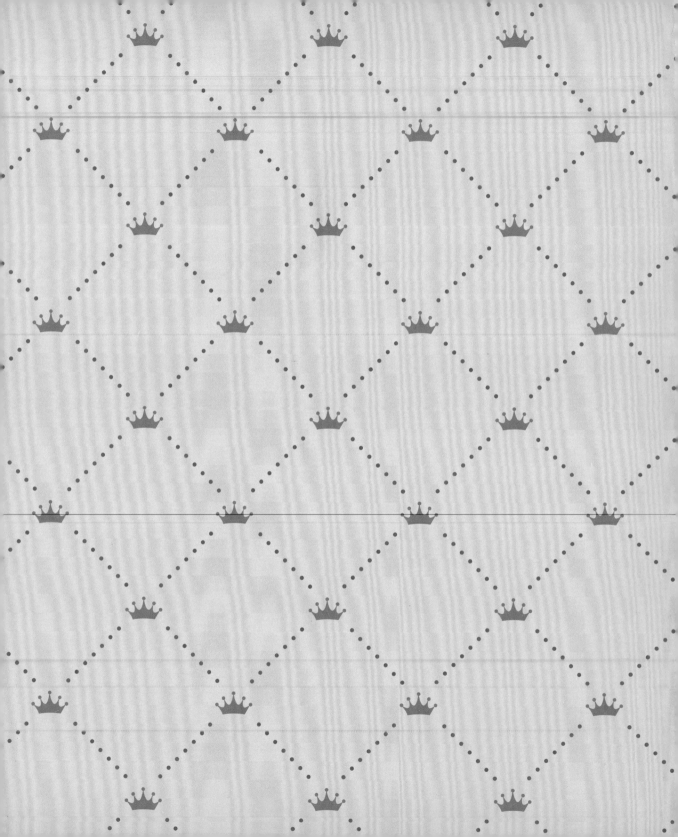